Workshop in a Box: Communication Skills for IT Professionals

Unlock the secrets of effective communication to transform
the way you interact and solve problems with your team,
and maximize the value of your IT skills

Abhinav Kaiser

Impackt Publishing

We Mean Business

Workshop in a Box: Communication Skills for IT Professionals

First published: April 2015

Production Reference: 1280415

Published by Impackt Publishing Ltd.
Livery Place
35 Livery Street
Birmingham B3 2PB, UK.

ISBN 978-1-78300-076-0

www.Impacktpub.com

Credits

Author
Abhinav Kaiser

Reviewer
M. S. Xavier Pradheep Singh

Acquisition Editor
Richard Gall

Content Development Editor
Amey Varangaonkar

Copy Editor
Sharvari H. Baet

Project Coordinator
Rashi Khivansara

Proofreaders
Simran Bhogal
Maria Gould
Paul Hindle
Vikrant Phadke

Graphics
Abhinash Sahu

Production Coordinator
Melwyn D'sa

Cover Work
Simon Cardew

About the Author

Abhinav Kaiser works as a Consulting Manager for a leading consulting firm. He has more than 12 years of experience in IT management consulting, IT management training, business process consulting, project management, transition management, and IT service management, among others.

He has helped organizations create value through IT, and has designed and implemented IT management solutions for smooth and efficient functioning of IT environments. He has trained thousands of IT professionals in soft skills and on management topics.

Abhinav has earned the Project Management Professional (PMP), ITIL Expert, and COBIT certifications. He blogs on communication and management on his weblog at `http://abhinavpmp.com`. His articles also appear on *Tech Republic* and *Pluralsight*.

He is from Bangalore, India and currently lives in Sydney, Australia. He is married and has a 5-year-old daughter.

I would like to first express my thanks to all my customers, without whom I would not have landed with rich and valuable experiences, stories, and incidents that have shaped every word in this book. Peers and friends likewise have been a part of the learning journey and still are. I would also like to thank my family who understood my additional responsibilities as an author, and ended up spending very less family time than usual. Lastly, I would like to thank Impackt Publishing for running with my idea, and supporting me through this journey.

About the Reviewer

M. S. Xavier Pradheep Singh has been teaching English language and literature at V. O. Chidambaram College, Tuticorin, Tamil Nadu, India, since 2009. His doctoral research was on enhancing English language skills through virtual learning environments. His areas of interest in teaching include communication skills, language skills, writing for print and web, and English language teaching.

Xavier is tech-savvy and is vigorously involved in researching and using technology innovatively in his classroom settings. He has also been a trainer in more than 15 workshops for English language teachers on computer-assisted language teaching organized by ELTAI, RELO, and IATEFL. He edits and reviews articles for the following journals, both in print and online: *Cuckoo*, *Journal of Teaching English with Technology*, *Journal of Technology for ELT*, *Journal of Teaching and Research in English Literature*, *Langlit*, and *Literary Voyage*. So far, Xavier has spoken in three international and seven national conferences on teacher education and web skills. His research articles have been published in various international journals, including, *Journal of NELTA* from Nepal, *Voices* from England, *ACJELL* from India, and *TEwT* from Poland.

With the help of a scholarship from the British Council, Xavier visited Bangladesh to participate in the Hornby Regional School held in Dhaka in 2011. He has completed two online teacher training courses offered by the University of Oregon, USA. More information on him is available at http://xavierpradheepxing.eu5.org. He can be contacted at pradheepxing@gmail.com. He posts blogs at http://pradheeponline.blogspot.in and shares his slideshows at http://www.slideshare.net/pradheepxing.

Contents

Chapter 3: Written Communication 35

Chapter 4: Listening and Questioning for Effective Communication 63

Chapter 7: Showcasing and Presentation   111

Chapter 8: Reports, Proposals, and Business Cases   129

Preface

How can I standardize communication across the organization? What can I do to ensure that my employees are productive and efficient? What measures should I take to keep the communication channels between employees and customers open and transparent? Why are so many conflicts creeping in every now and then?

The solutions to these problems are in this book. Many organizations concentrate on honing technical skills and give little importance to communication. It is a fact that employees spend more time communicating than doing their respective core activities. In this scenario, not giving communication improvement due consideration is an opportunity wasted when it comes to getting the most out of them.

In today's competitive world, communication in business is no longer simply regarded as a humble "soft skill" that is an extension of the employee's primary skills. The importance of communication skills is such that it is perhaps now a skill that is valued more than, say, technical and management skills. Of course, technical expertise is essential, but with an increasingly educated workforce leaving university, there should be—in theory at least—a wealth of talent for organizations to choose from. Great communication skills can make an individual stand out, and can make them an invaluable member of a team.

It is certainly worthwhile putting in the time and effort to develop your team's skills; whether someone considers themselves a great communicator or they readily admit that communication is not their forte, there is always room to improve! Before you begin to develop your communication skills or help others develop theirs, it is essential to get a grounding in the basics of communication. Getting to the heart of the matter and understanding exactly what is going on every time you communicate is the first step to being a great communicator.

This book aims to help you out in running your own workshop with your teams, rather than bringing in a consultant like me, which is bound to be expensive. Also, you will have the flexibility of running it a number of times, anytime, and at locations of your choice. Through this book, you can readily fix your current communication structure and take measures to make communication between teams effective and reap the benefits of increased productivity.

When I go out on consulting assignments, I have witnessed firsthand that the right hand of an organization doesn't talk to the left hand. They are left hanging in between, and this results in a great amount of rework and a substantial increase in operating costs. In one case, a team was carrying out their work but never bothered to update anybody, nor did they have any system of logging what they did. This led to panicky stakeholders who had to chase up multiple times. Consequently, managers of this team did not have any clue whether job was done or not. They ended up acting as middlemen between the engineers on the floor and customers. This in turn resulted in a lot of wasted time in getting the update and passing it on to the customer. This is where I came in and introduced a system where the customers were able to obtain updates by themselves on a real-time basis by logging in to a portal. The onus was on the engineers to keep the status updates posted whenever there was something substantial to report. This solution ensured that customers got what they wanted, and the organization serving them could effectively manage expectations and communications through real-time reporting.

IT is becoming an increasingly large part of business life—although IT departments may have been secondary to an organization's operations and strategy in the past, in today's highly connected and digitized environment, they are the lifeblood of a business. IT departments certainly have more responsibility than they have ever had before. I have written this book keeping IT as the focus, although it can be used with any other non-IT teams as well. In fact, this book should be used by managers who head IT teams and who are ready to run their own workshops to improve communication—end to end.

I did not study communication in college. My academic background is in engineering and I currently work as a consultant. This book is an outcome of the education I have gained during my consulting experience, and from my cognizance of existing communication systems in organizations. During the course of the workshop, I will throw light on some relevant real-life examples. I am certain that you will be able to relate to a number of cases that I discuss, which will help you bring up the cases during your training sessions.

What you will learn in this book

Chapter 1, Communication Training, introduces a number of topics related to communication, quality, and training. This chapter acts as a launchpad for running the workshop.

Chapter 2, From Governance to Communication, equips you with all the tools and techniques necessary to run the workshop, including templates, checklists, and all other accessories.

Chapter 3, Written Communication, looks at written communication and its various flavors—e-mails, mailers, notifications, visuals, infographics, and process maps.

Chapter 4, Listening and Questioning for Effective Communication, gives you all of the ammunition you need to be an effective communicator, without which the shallowness of your communication stands exposed.

Chapter 5, Telephone Communication, specifically looks at communicating over the telephone. We discuss the importance of listening before speaking and tips for improving listening skills.

Chapter 6, Face-to-face Communication, discusses the nuances of face-to-face communication. This chapters hovers around the various channels that exist in face-to-face communication, voice intonations, and facial expressions.

Chapter 7, Showcasing and Presentation, looks at presentation and showcasing skills, which includes displaying confidence during meetings, presentations, and seminars.

Chapter 8, Reports, Proposals, and Business Cases, shows you how you can go about preparing reports in the most logical manner. We also break down business proposals and see how they need to be developed to get the attention of prospective customers.

To succeed, we need to be protagonists of championing quality in every field of our work, study, and hobbies. In every chapter, I have introduced quality checks that you can perform to vet whether the objectives of the chapter have been met. Although a number of things could sound repetitive, it is in your best interest to review the objectives of every chapter.

Who this book is for

This book is for anyone who works in technical fields and wants to develop their communication skills. If you want to develop better working relationships, communicate your ideas more effectively, and build a wider culture of collaboration and understanding, this book is for you. Most, if not all, businesses rate time management as one of the most important skills in their employees. Good time management leads to better productivity and profitability. Training in time management will enable businesses be more efficient and effective. This book is targeted at three groups of individuals. It is designed to bring a new employee up to speed in time management. It will also help managers guide their teams, especially new hires, in time management just as a master craftsman guides apprentices. Finally, it will serve as reference material for trainers and coaches who offer time management courses.

Conventions

In this book, you will find a number of styles of text that distinguish between different kinds of information. Here are some examples of these styles, and an explanation of their meaning.

New terms and **important words** are shown in bold.

	For Reference
	For Reference appear like this

	Lists
	Lists appear like this

	Action Point
	Action points appear like this

	Make a note
	Warnings or important notes appear in a box like this.

	Tip
	Tips and tricks appear like this.

Reader feedback

Feedback from our readers is always welcome. Let us know what you think about this book—what you liked or may have disliked. Reader feedback is important for us to develop titles that you really get the most out of.

To send us general feedback, simply send an e-mail to feedback@impacktpub.com, and mention the book title via the subject of your message.

If there is a topic that you have expertise in and you are interested in either writing or contributing to a book, see our author guide on www.impacktpub.com/authors.

Customer support

Now that you are the proud owner of an Impackt book, we have a number of things to help you to get the most from your purchase.

Errata

Although we have taken every care to ensure the accuracy of our content, mistakes do happen. If you find a mistake in one of our books—maybe a mistake in the text—we would be grateful if you would report this to us. By doing so, you can save other readers from frustration and help us improve subsequent versions of this book. If you find any errata, please report them by visiting http://www.impacktpub.com/support, selecting your book, clicking on the **errata submission form** link, and entering the details of your errata. Once your errata are verified, your submission will be accepted and the errata will be uploaded on our website, or added to any list of existing errata, under the Errata section of that title. Any existing errata can be viewed by selecting your title from http://www.impacktpub.com/support.

Piracy

Piracy of copyright material on the Internet is an ongoing problem across all media. At Impackt, we take the protection of our copyright and licenses very seriously. If you come across any illegal copies of our works, in any form, on the Internet, please provide us with the location address or website name immediately so that we can pursue a remedy.

Please contact us at copyright@impacktpub.com with a link to the suspected pirated material.

We appreciate your help in protecting our authors, and our ability to bring you valuable content.

Questions

You can contact us at questions@impacktpub.com if you are having a problem with any aspect of the book, and we will do our best to address it.

>1

Communication Training

In an increasingly digitized and computerized world, the image of the solitary IT worker is rapidly disappearing; this may be as much an image change as the truth, but one cannot deny that communication skills are becoming increasingly important for IT teams.

Nobody can work in silos. Although coding jobs make programmers sit in isolated cubicles with computer monitors stuck to their faces, their lines of code will eventually have to talk to other lines of code that are developed by other programmers. Work cannot happen in isolation; products and services are a result of joint efforts. The collaboration effort will ensure success and the binding factor that brings in the collaborating elements together is communication.

For example, a customer might say that he needs a light colored website with an option to blog and a shopping cart among other items. What the customer wants and how well the project manager grasps the requirements is dependent on the effectiveness of the communication between the customer and the project manager. If the customer has excellent communication skills and if the project manager is a terrible listener, requirements take a hit and this results in the end product being out of sync. Once the project manager understands the requirements accurately, they will have to cascade this information to the rest of their team—where once again communication skills come into play. In this way, every instance of collaboration is held together by communication.

The following figure has become a meme in project management circles. It depicts the breakdown of communication in a project. What a customer wants and what they eventually get are like the flipsides of a coin. Everyone has their own vision, unconcerned with the customer and without any alignment with others:

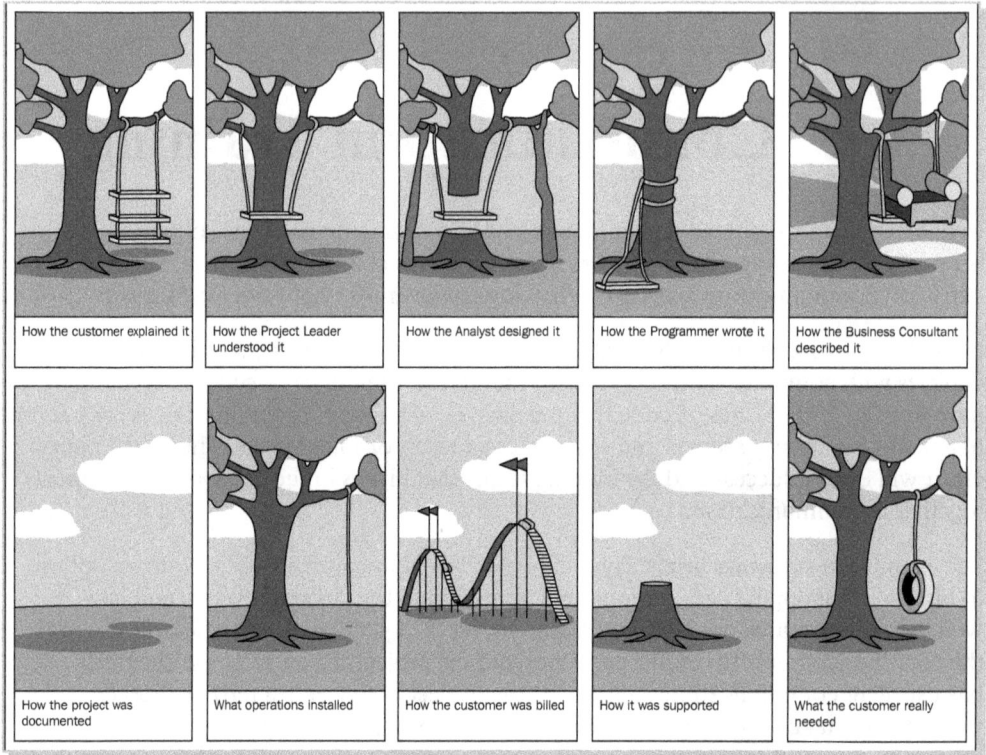

| How the customer explained it | How the Project Leader understood it | How the Analyst designed it | How the Programmer wrote it | How the Business Consultant described it |
| How the project was documented | What operations installed | How the customer was billed | How it was supported | What the customer really needed |

It is this unity between departments and the respective roles within departments that ensures that individual tasks, larger projects, and even larger business objectives are met.

It is this issue that should lie at the heart of the development of your staff's communication skills—good communication should not simply be desired for itself, but is rather instrumental in getting effective results. Thinking of communication skills as "soft" is a little misleading, as if they are not really tied to the "hard facts" of business. The truth is, they are; good communication skills absolutely impact the bottom line.

How to use this communication training guide

Communication is a major risk affecting IT organizations worldwide. To mitigate it, employees need to be trained on various aspects of communication, the dos, don'ts, etiquettes and other related areas of study. Since the recession of early 2000s, organizations are looking to cut costs, and increase productivity to survive in the competitive IT market. One of the areas where most organizations have stopped funding is in the training function. These days, companies expect employees to self-learn and apply the results at work. The days of companies sponsoring and nurturing employees are long gone. This is precisely the area where this book comes into play. It benefits organizations to run their own training sessions with minimal preparation, and employees are treated to valuable on-the-job training that is relevant to the work they perform and the knowledge gained here can boost their performance and thrust their careers into new horizons. This book can be used:

> **As a training guide:** Due to the decentralized learning functions in companies, we have designed this guide for team managers to act as trainers who can impart the knowledge contained in this book. This guide consists of exercises that trainers can readily apply at the end of sessions, and incorporated exercises provide thought-provoking topics that will help teams come together and brainstorm ideas discussed in the book.

> **As a self-study material:** The book can also be used as self-help study material. Employees can read and understand the material on their own, perform individual exercises, and get together at least once a week to discuss the topics. The uncomplicated flow and structure of this guide can be just as easily digested by the employees themselves. And, it could potentially be as effective as a trainer led course as long as they work on the exercises and discuss the topics as a group.

Strategy for trainers

One of my professional roles is that of a corporate trainer. I train IT people in a classroom setting, and there are a few things I have learned along that way that has helped me develop as a better trainer than when I started out. I am going to share a couple of tools that are most useful, and they are result-bound. These tools are:

> **Relate training aspects to life activities:** Make any training interesting by relating it back to the trainees, something that they can relate to on a day-to-day basis. Suppose you want to teach a topic on listening, start with a real-life illustration, say employees communicating with their girlfriends and boyfriends and how various conflicts arise out of not listening to one another before responding. At this point, you will know that you have connected with your trainees from the number of nodding heads agreeing with what you mentioned, and this is a sign that you have struck a chord. At this point, bring the focus back to office work, and map it to the activities they perform. Say, for example, customer complaints arising out of not understanding their problems. Voila, you have successfully mapped a topic on communication directly to work activities, and trust me, the understanding of the topic has been effective as well.

> **Indulge in role play:** Another tool that you can employ during the training is role play. Develop a few roles that employees can enact in front of others, the roles staying relevant to the topic. Through role play, you are showing rather than saying it out loud. Prompt where necessary to drive the role play in the intended direction and to get the most out of it. Role play can be considered as result-oriented as the live everyday examples.

Quality in communication

When you go shopping for a product, say a television, you would invariably want to get the most value for your money, in layman's terms—you want a quality product. Have you thought of what the word quality means to you? The fact is that the term quality can have multiple definitions depending on the context. There is no one single definition that can be attributed to quality. Meets the requirements, does what it is supposed to, works well for a number of years, suits my need perfectly, and there are many more suitors. In the case of the television, I would define quality as picture in high definition resolution, crisp and clear audio, and the product must last at least five years without any maintenance in between. As I mentioned earlier, quality means different things to different people. Ask yourself or your neighbor what quality means to them in relation to buying a television. They will give you a separate list of requirements and definitions.

When you go hunting for a professional training session, you would like to get a hang on everything there is to the subject you are intending to be trained in—in other words you are looking for quality training. Have you ever thought of what the word quality means to you? The word quality can have different meanings depending on the context. I cannot state a single sentence to define quality. Some IT professionals may relate quality training to the depth of knowledge that was imparted and some might give importance to the content that helps them get certifications. If you ask me what quality means, I would say that it should impart in-depth knowledge of the subject, provide sufficient examples for me to understand the concepts with ease, and if a certification is involved the focus should be on strategies to answer the certification exam. You might have a completely different expectation of what quality training is.

How can you differentiate a quality product from a non-quality one? The answer is improvement, not just once but on a regular basis. Regular improvements go by a Japanese word **kaizen,** which stands for continuous improvement. Kaizen ensures that the products and services are bound by continuous improvement, even if the improvement is miniscule. By improving continuously, products and services are always a notch or two ahead of the rest.

In communication, kaizen has a special meaning. The effectiveness of communication and the productivity must be improved on a regular basis. As individuals, you must always try to improve your communication skills by understanding and implementing the *7 Cs* in your personal and work life, understand your own communication style and that of others who you regularly communicate with and make a conceited effort in building rapport with people who matter. This is not a one-time activity; you need to keep doing this as and when the situation demands it. To state an example, you can run this workshop multiple times, and the effectiveness in communication is bound to increase by a percentage every time you run it. Perhaps you can improvise by adding customized exercises based on your organization's cases. The underlying principle is that such workshops, whether they are on communication or any other topic, is not a standalone activity, but a process that has to be imbibed into the DNA of the organization.

Let's see what other aspects could render communication as a quality product or otherwise. Communication is of quality if it is effective in:

➤ Transmitting the message in verbatim to the receiver (integrity)

➤ Understanding the message in verbatim by the recipient as the sender intends

➤ Presenting the message concisely and to the point without any unnecessary text in the message

➤ Understanding the message easily

➤ Providing due consideration to all recipients it is intends to reach

➤ Being courteous and taking the cross-cultural attributes into play

➤ Reaching the recipient at the time it was intended to

When you start to answer the question of what quality means to you in communication, you could come up with an entirely different set, plus or minus the set I have put forth. For me, if my communication can meet my quality requirements as stated here, then I can subsequently consider it to be precisely that—quality. This quality message serves as a baseline, from which I could then begin to work on the principle of kaizen through one of the methods that I discuss in the next section, *The PDCA circle*.

The PDCA circle

The PDCA circle is a popular model in practicing continuous improvement or kaizen. PDCA abbreviates to a four activity iterative approach—plan, do, check, and act:

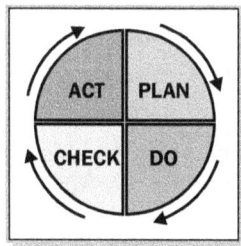

```
ACT    PLAN
CHECK  DO
```

This concept was tested in the real world and made popular by William Edwards Deming, and it is also commonly known as the **Deming cycle**. The cycle was, however, theorized by Walter Stewhart, and Deming during his years in Japan referred to the cycle as the Stewhart cycle.

When you create a new product, it is likely that it is far from perfect. However, you will probably have a basic or vague understanding of what perfect looks like. So, you start taking baby steps towards the perfection through the use of PDCA cycle. You will get to the point of near perfection as you keep making incremental and nonstop improvements. You can see your product evolve in every step of the way. Most, if not all, organizations use this methodology to make their products or services the best they can possibly be. Apple products did not come out chiseled the way they seem to be.

They grew slowly through multiple iterations of improvements, adding one feature at a time and one product launch after another. PDCA plays a major role in industries where the time to market is as long as the lifespan of a housefly. Let me take you through the individual stages of the PDCA cycle:

➤ **Plan:** Chart out your objectives, goals, and targets that you wish to achieve in a given period of time. The planning stage gives you the direction for improvements and tells you how quickly and how swiftly you need to proceed towards the intended target. To do this stage effectively, you need to have the vision to see things from afar, which could be weeks, months, or even years. Every new product you get in the market is designed during the planning stage and then the team of developers bring the design on paper to life.

In communication, you need to plan your communication channels, policies, processes, and style guides among others. It is important to know that the communication planning plays a key role in ensuring that information is exchanged effectively and efficiently as well. Also, it can be done economically through the use of technologies such as VOIP and e-mails.

➤ **Do:** In this stage, you start executing your plans. In the design of a cell phone, let's say that the planning stage came up with the concept of haptic feedback in theory. Developers in the "do" stage will look to breathe life into the design and make it a reality. To summarize, in this stage the actual implementation or deployment takes place, as specified in the planning stage.

The output of the planning stage—various planning documents such as policies, controls, and procedures are implemented in the doing stage. Implementation of communication controls will include training the employees, letting customers and vendors know of the frequencies and mediums that will be used and perhaps hand-holding employees, customers, users, and vendors to carry out the necessary communication-related activities.

➤ **Check:** At this stage, you have a plan and it has been achieved as well. To what extent the plan has been achieved is the objective of the check stage. While the designs are given shape during the "do" stage, it is common to sway from the target—meaning the specifications might not be met. People working on projects can get blinded by the proximity they are in. But, when you take a step back and observe the progress, you will be in a good position to judge where we are in terms of achieving the goals put out in the plan stage. The "check" stage will analyze the product or service and compare it to the specification document from the plan stage, and then produce a delta analysis that basically tells all stakeholders what else needs to be achieved to attain the desired specifications.

When we implement communication policy and procedures, say by training employees, some may get it and some won't. It is also possible that the infrastructure does not support the communication needs or the users just don't feel like following the new rules around communication. In such cases, as an analyst, you would make observations on where things are not going as per plan and how they need to be tweaked.

➤ **Act:** At this point, you have a gap analysis document in your hand listing the delta between desired and achieved. The next stage is rather logical and predictable, right? You act on the shortcomings to meet the desired results. In the corporate world, when new operating systems such as Android are rolled out, you see a number of updates roll in from time to time. These updates are coming from your act stage and are molding the sculpture slowly but surely. If you look around, you can find a number of examples that are living act stages in play.

The same goes for communication. Plug all the gaps and ensure that the plan comes to fruition by fulfilling the requirements.

➤ **The Iteration:** The plan-do-check-act process that I took you through is considered a single cycle. You need to do it as many number of times as the product or service is live. The preceding figure shows you how multiple iterations improve the quality of the object and takes it towards perfection. The x axis is represented by time and y axis is represented by quality. As time progresses, you can get in more PDCA iterations, which leads to quality improvement—the objective of the Deming cycle.

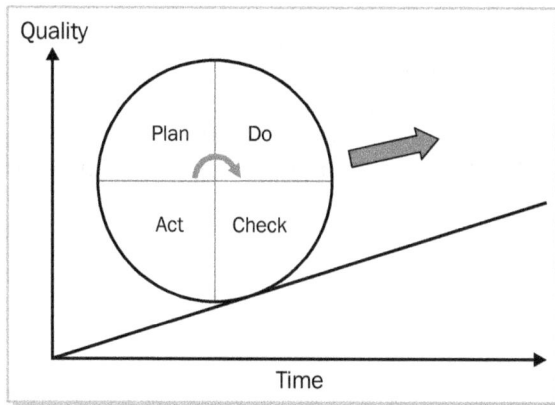

➤ **Applicability:** As I mentioned earlier, you can apply PDCA to any area and it is bound to produce positive results, including the area of your personal life where you can set yourself goals to achieve and work towards achieving them. After you think you have achieved them, compare them with your goals and identify the delta. Work towards bridging the gap and repeat the cycle as long as you are competitive to improve on a continuous basis. It works!

I used the example of a product mainly to explain the concept of PDCA. Apart from products, service industries can leverage on it too to improve the services they provide—potential areas could be IT services, hospitality, utilities and so on. You would definitely need to rely on this model if you are looking to bring about improvements into projects. I can probably go on for the next few pages on the industries where the Deming cycle would be applicable and still have a few more pages left. I will not do this, and instead hope that you understand the depth and compatibility with various systems, objects, and processes.

In this workshop, you will see PDCA in action. You will plan the workshop and then run the training to your employees and at the end of every chapter there is an assessment test provided. This test is a good reflector of how well your students understand the topics of this workshop. If you find the results of the assessment unsatisfactory, take a step back, and find another way to train them on the topics where they didn't score well. This way, you are not just delivering the training, but checking the understanding and doing what is necessary to bridge the gap.

Summary

As this chapter ends, you are expected to know the following:

> ➤ How the training guide can be used
> ➤ Strategies for trainers
> ➤ The concept of quality in communication
> ➤ The PDCA circle

In the next chapter, we will look into how companies are organized and dissect the term governance and its impact on communication, along with the communication process. We will delve into the basics of communication, the styles of communication, conflicts that could arise out of communication, and the importance of relationships and rapport to make communication effective and productive. In short, a number of exciting topics await you!

>2

From Governance
to Communication

At a most basic level, communication is the exchange of information. There is a source who is the originator of the information and the recipient who is expected to receive it. Typically, communication happens between:

> A sender to a receiver (closed room discussion between manager and subordinate)

> A sender to multiple receivers (a speaker talking at a seminar)

> Multiple senders to a single receiver (e-mails from a number of people dropping into my inbox)

> Multiple senders to multiple receivers (meetings or a group discussion setting)

Apart from the information exchange, the media or the form through which communication exchanges happen is relevant as well. The person sending the information may choose one medium over the other, for example, a telephone call over sending out an e-mail. Every form of communication has its advantages and disadvantages as well. We will discuss the various types of communication and the pros and cons of each type. This communication training guide will help you and your team choose the medium to opt for during various situations.

Communication and organizational structure

I once attended a seminar where one of the speakers, representing project managers, emphasized that communication is most important to managers as they are the people who act as a bond between the senior members of an organization and the wider workforce. They are required to translate business requirements into project activities, report on the project statuses to the customer, and liaise with vendors.

As I thought more about the speech, it made me realize that the speaker was missing the hidden truth about communication in the workplace—there is no central power base, but a complex web of interactions, all of which need to be treated seriously. Many organizations follow a pyramid structure of hierarchy, where staff at a lower level outnumber their superiors; it seems utterly crazy that the core of communication should be confined to such a small cross-section of an organization's structure. If the bottom half of the organization makes up most of your organization, how can the project manager at the seminar claim that communication is most important to managers?

In any organization, the communication channel from top to bottom must flow and be error free so that the communication regarding activities taking place at the ground level flows to the top uninterrupted and without distortion. For the pyramid to hold tight, the movement of communication needs to be an infinitely more complex web than the simple top-down structure that appears to be in place in much thinking. Communication is critical to all parts of the organization and organizations must make every effort to improve communication in all directions and for all parties—not just those leading operations. While we reason that communication must be effective at all levels of the organization, companies don't often focus on providing their employees with quality communication training. They expect their employees to communicate clearly and accurately, but don't do enough to build the foundation to bring them up to speed. Companies must invariably impart communication training, not only to those at the management positions but also to all layers—starting from the bottom layer and moving upstream.

Communication and governance

Governance is about leadership, oversight, and consistent management in organizations. The decisions made by the governance body binds the organization together in reaching a targeted objective—in our case, the governance body has decided to improve the communication skillsets of IT employees, and has employed the services of this training guide. It is therefore fair to state that the development of communication starts budding with the seeds planted in the governance layer. The decisions undertaken trickle down from the governance through various layers of the organization to the targeted group—employees.

In fact, most enterprises these days have treaded this path with a documented communication policy that acts as a bible when it comes to communicating across mediums, roles, layers, vendors, and customers. To ensure that the elements of the policy are acted out, several communication-training sessions are held and feedback from managers obtained on a regular basis.

Before we move any further, let me justify the reasons for bringing up governance in a communication book. As you are aware, the objective of this book is to improve communication in your organization, especially from an IT department standpoint. Improved communication results in increased effectiveness of information exchange. For communication to be effective, you need to have a proper grounding, a sturdy foundation laid for it to stand the test of time and circumstances. At this point, we are expecting governance to be in place for training employees on communication skills, and hence the decision to use this guide to improve the communication of IT employees.

If you wanted to make changes in middle management, for example, there are good chances that your own employees might not buy the idea of the (positive) change you bring in. So you invariably need the blessings of the governance body. If the body is in favor of changes, it trickles down one layer at a time and the end result gets accepted by all employees without a question being asked.

Communication policy

One of the key instruments for effective governance is an effective policy. In terms of communication, a good policy will lay the groundwork and provide guidelines that enable organizational unity so everyone is working towards a shared goal. The policy should be at the forefront of your mind when training your employees, just as it should be at the forefront of your employees' minds when they are communicating.

The purpose of a communication policy is to introduce mechanisms of accountability, and to make employees responsible for delivering on their targets. It provides guidance, but it also creates a barometer from which performance can be measured. It reaches out to specific groups of employees and demarcates the scope of the policy in black and white. A policy document should be directive and clear. It is a common sight these days to break up communication into various manageable pieces, and every piece having a policy of its own. Examples of this range from a board of directors' communication policy, an e-mail policy, wireless communication policy, internal communication policy, and customer communication policy. This is not comprehensive but a sample to taste the varying wavelengths of policy documents. Every policy will serve a definite purpose, and ideally, there must not be any overlaps.

While training employees using this guide, policies play a pivotal role in orienting employees to the objectives that are to be achieved through the aid of directions set in it. Organizations vary in terms of their values and principles, and this has a bearing on the policy documents—including the communication policy document. By basing the training on the organization's policy, the training is customized to the needs and requirements of the company, and it isn't just generic training available off the shelves of a bookstore.

I have drafted a sample policy document that illustrates what a communication policy could look like. In my example, I have included a few sub sections such as objective, scope, and ownership, among others. There is no hard and fast rule that a policy document must look a certain way, but it is important for you and your employees to be aware of the policies as you seek to help them develop their skills.

Sample communication policy

The following image is a sample of the communication policy:

Purpose

The purpose of this communication policy is to bring in standardization of communication to customers.

Scope

This policy applies to all communications made by employees to external customers in the following modes:

- E-mail
- Reports and
- Presentations

Ownership

Respective business unit heads will own implementation of this policy in their respective business units.

Accesses

- Customer information must be access controlled, and the BU head will grant approval for getting the access.
- All e-mails must be sent through the organization's internal exchange server only.
- E-mails to external domains is permitted on demand only. Provide the customer domain name, and obtain access to send emails to customer email addresses. Approver is BU head.

Format

- Latest organization templates must be used for preparing reports.
- E-mails to be sent in HTML format with white background.
- All e-mails must have company assigned signature at the end of the email message.
- All e-mails must contain a subject line and address the customer using respective salutation.
- Meeting requests must be accompanied by a clearly thought out agenda, meeting notes from previous meetings (if any) and a timeline as agreed by all parties.

Data Sharing

- Information must be shared through e-mails only.
- Smaller files must be attached in an e-mail and larger e-mails must be shared only through our file transfer protocol system.
- All files shared with customers must be in protected PDF format only.

Changes to Policy

Feedback on this policy document is encouraged and expected of all employees. If you want to suggest changes or improvements, send an e-mail to policyfeedback@companyabcxyz.com.

Action Point

Exercise (for readers to attempt at the end of this topic followed by a group discussion):

- Identify the existing policies in your organization and compare them with the sample communication policy (in terms of format and style).
- If you were to develop your own communication policy, how would you do it? Use the sample communication policy as the base.
- Discuss how a communication policy can impact your organization with respect to standardization.

The communication process

Policies define boundaries, set rules, and give the direction for an individual or group to take within an organization. A process, meanwhile, addresses the means of achieving the objective as directed by the policy. A process can be defined as a series of coordinated actions aimed towards achieving a preset goal. For a process, there are inputs, a trigger to set it in motion and an objective that it needs to achieve or you could call it the output of a process. It is the policy in action.

The idea of a "process" can be elucidated with the following example:

> *You are told by your manager that a weekly project report needs to be sent out to the customer from the following week. Preparing a report is a process, as there is a series of interconnected activities that string together to bring out specific output.*

In this example, the manager's instructions got you started on preparing the report, so this becomes the trigger for the process. A process needs inputs to churn out the required end result. In this case, the project status is the input. The project status could read something like coding development activity complete, testing activity to start next week, and vendor negotiations to be closed next week. The output of these activities is the weekly report which gets published to the customer.

The process for this activity could look something like this:

1. Bring in all the team leaders on a call on Friday evening
2. Obtain an update from each of the teams
3. Using the existing project report template, populate the project updates
4. Get the report reviewed by the project manager and e-mail the report to the customer

This is a four-step process and after completing the final action, you will have achieved your intended goal, however simple it may be. The definition of a process states that it is a series of interconnected actions to achieve your result. So in effect, none of the four steps could be interchanged with another to achieve the same result. This means that you cannot get the weekly report approved before creating it. It needs to happen in a sequence. The sequence of events is the process that will help take you towards the objectives you wish to achieve, be it sending out a report or making communication effective and efficient.

As a consultant, one of my primary jobs is to develop processes for my customers. My customers (generally) are aware what they need to achieve, and they have the resources to make it a reality. I fill in the important role by defining the activities, assigning responsibilities, and ensuring the process delivers on its promise. It is in the process layer where efficiency, effectiveness, optimization, and cost-cutting are achieved.

How does a process help in the development of communication?

A well-defined process helps you standardize communication across your organization. Customers or any of the stakeholders for that matter will not see a distinct difference in communication when different people in the organization are involved in it. They see the organization as one unit and not the peaks and troughs that are generally visible from one employee to another. A well-defined process has the potential to take feedback, tweak the process for the better, and improve on effectiveness and productivity.

Communication is complicated and convoluted given the mediums, cultural differences, and subtleties it brings in and can be considered a giant. The only way you can control it is by breaking it part by part. Any complex activity can be broken down into manageable pieces.

When the individual activities are broken down, the rule of thumb is that every individual activity must have input and output. Let's say you want to prepare a business case. Business case by itself can be daunting but not if you break it down into individual parts that can be interlinked with one another. For a business case, let us assume that the individual activities involved are:

➤ Identification of value

➤ Organizing information

➤ Putting together the ideas in the form of a document

➤ Review the document to see if it follows the intended pattern

So, when you are trying to simplify a complex activity, say a business case that needs to be sent out to your manager, you need to identify the individual parts. For every individual part, identify what goes into the activity and what comes out. By linking individual activities with one another, you get the process that will give you the intended solution.

Sample communication process

In this section, let's look at a sample communication process workflow. This process workflow will serve as an example of how a process will look in the real world, and the concept can be better taught through this example. The workflow illustrated here is a typical scenario in IT companies where users call the support engineers to have their queries answered. Let's see how this may work out.

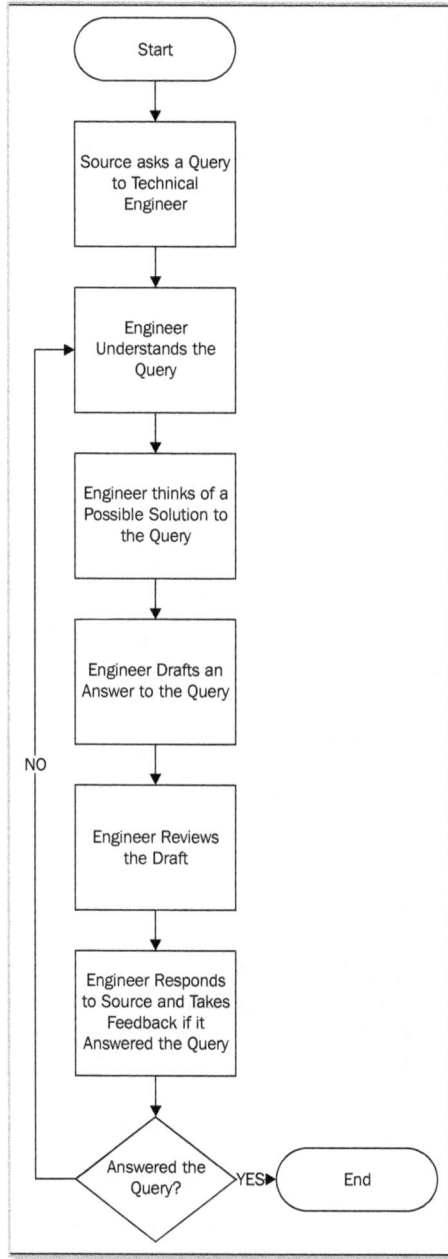

In this process, the key points are as follows:

1. The recipient tries to understand the query, perhaps going through the query multiple times to ensure they got it right.

2. After apprehending the request from the source, the engineer comes up with a befitting solution that will meet the requirements of the source.

3. Before the engineer transmits the message back to source, the message is vetted against meeting the requirements and for possible errors.

4. After transmitting the message to source, the engineer asks for feedback on whether the answer fulfilled the requirements. If the feedback from the source suggests that it did not meet the requirements, the loop traces back to the engineer understanding the requirements.

There are some key points borne out of this example that are worth bearing in mind throughout the workshop. They are as follows:

➤ Do not assume that you have understood the requirements. Go back and double-check whether you have understood the requirements. The key to effectiveness and efficiency is to not rework activities due to human errors (such as responding back to the customer before fully understanding the requirement), unless it is beyond our control. This is illustrated in the process activity where the engineer first understands the query before responding back.

➤ As a manager, you should frown on errors but at the same time provide controls for sufficient quality checks before the delivery is made. This is illustrated in the review deliverable activity before sending it to the customer.

➤ Feedback is the breakfast of champions. Performing individuals in their respective fields are highly placed because they value feedback and act on them. The workshop will be a closed loop system, meaning that the feedback mechanism will be an integral part of it. As feedback asks the question—how am I doing? Can I do it better? And most importantly, it feels the pulse of the opposite party who is communicating. The recipient can tell you how you fared and provide pointers. You can use this feedback and build on it to improve communication skills and related activities.

➤ The feedback mechanism provides us with the opportunity to improve quality (discussed in detail later in this chapter). After performing the activity, take a step back and check whether it conforms to requirements. The feedback activity as well as the review process activity helps us with the continuous quality improvement portions of the workshop. Whatever activity you perform, whether it's a soft skill such as communication or a technical one, take feedback whether what you have achieved is satisfactory or not. The feedback you get is priceless. The appraisal system that is conducted in most enterprises follow this pattern. First, your manager tries to evaluate you by asking for a self-assessment and then provides their feedback. The idea is to check whether you are aware of where you stand, and then share feedback from their perspective.

Action Point

Exercise (for readers to attempt at the end of this topic followed by a group discussion):

- Do you believe that introducing processes in your organization will benefit in streamlining activities and improving productivity? Use existing organizational processes to build on this discussion.

- If you were to develop your own communication process, how would you do it? Use the sample communication process as the base. Identify an existing communication channel in your organization (say, instant messaging) for developing a process.

Basics of communication

While official policies and processes are essential for good communication, the individual skills of employees are where great communication happens. Policies and procedures are nothing on their own—only by having the necessary skills can their requirements be fulfilled. If great communication was as easy as following rules and edicts it would be easy, and you probably wouldn't need this book. Yet we need policies and processes in place to create a suitable environment for communication training to be aligned with the organization's goals and stay effective and consistent. The next few sections will provide an overview of the core ideas of communication and its applicability to IT organizations.

The rest of this chapter is designed in a self-help model where readers can study the topics and understand the concepts on their own. The requirement of a trainer to go through the basics of communication is optional. Each section has exercises built into it, and we encourage group discussions to be held during and after completing the exercises. The outcome of the exercises could be used to assess understanding.

7 Cs of effective communication

In IT organizations, where time is money and effectiveness is value, getting communication right is key. It doesn't have to be complicated, though—the 7 Cs of communication gives you the most important points in an easy alliterative list.

In many cases, there are no second chances especially when communicating with customers, so it is imperative that employees who are undergoing this training acknowledge the importance of these basic ideas—eventually, it will become second nature and habitual.

Whatever situation you or your team find yourselves in, the 7 Cs provide a good baseline from which to develop communication skills.

Action Point

Exercise

- A very useful preliminary task in the training is to get your team talking about the 7 Cs of communication. Get them to give examples of each of the Cs in action. First get them to give an imagined example, and then get them to think of an instance when this applies to them in their own work.

Completeness

Suppose you deliver a demonstration on how to operate a kitchen product; if the audience has too many questions at the end of your talk, it may be safe to assume that the demonstration was not complete. If the answers to the questions were included in the demonstration, you would spend a lot less time than you would to answering everyone's questions. If you are complete in your communication this will save you time, ultimately making you—and hopefully those around you — a lot more productive.

Conciseness

Communication needs to be complete, but it must also be *concise*. Keep the exchange of information minimal, but do not compromise its value.

All communication has certain limits placed on it—whether it is time, space, or even effort. There is effectively always some kind of bandwidth when you communicate, even in nondigital scenarios! Keep your use of bandwidth at a minimum, as this will ensure that communication is efficient. You could look at it from another angle. Mistakes or distortion in communication is directly proportional to the length of the message, just like the defect rate in manufacturing. The longer the message, the more the mistakes, hence the degradation in quality of communication. All the more reason to root for conciseness.

Consideration

In training sessions, I am likely to have a diverse group of people, in terms of work experience. I can have vice presidents of organizations, managers, software developers, network administrators, and fresh recruits as trainees in the same class. When I teach, I need to give due *consideration* to all the trainees by either scaling up or scaling down the teaching methodology. Why do I need to scale up or scale down based on the audience? Because I need to take my audience into consideration. I need to understand whether they are following me. If they don't follow me, there is no meaning to what I teach, and the training is not effective.

If you are to be an effective communicator, you need to understand your audience. You need to step into the shoes of your recipients. You need to ask questions such as is this message making sense to whomever I am sending it to? Is it relevant? Is it adding value to what they already know? Am I carrying coal to New Castle (repeating known information)? These questions are not comprehensive but you get the idea. Right?

Concreteness

It goes without saying that the message originator must understand the objective of a particular exchange of information, and ensure that the message is straightforward and not ambiguous. Whenever you are making a point, be sure to justify it with examples, facts, and figures. Justification helps in gaining the confidence of the recipient which is the crux for getting your intended message across.

Courtesy

All forms of communication need to involve and engage the other; whether you are talking directly to someone or sending an e-mail, you need to interact with your interlocutor with warmth and friendliness. Negativity should be avoided—this does not mean you should avoid certain issues, but rather that even if you are dealing with a problem, this needs to be done in a positive way. The best example here is feedback—feedback should be about thinking about particular problems and working through criticisms, but it should never purely critical and negative.

Be sensitive to the situation and be sensitive to the recipient—even if the blame lies with them. Being harsh does no good, but showing signs of positivity can move things forward effectively.

Clearness

Clarity is an essential component of great communication. It is closely related to conciseness—your message needs to be easily understood. The recipient will not laud you for the excellent language you have used, and the innumerable unknown words that you have used. They want to understand what you are trying to convey in the simplest possible way by following the path of the least resistance.

Correctness

Errors bring down the quality of a message. The recipient loses confidence in your communication if they identify errors. Extra care must be taken that whatever you are communicating is free of errors. There are, of course, two ways of understanding *errors*—the content of the communication or its form and the way it is communicated. For excellent communication, you need to be sure that you are accurate in your information and the way you express yourself.

Action Point

Exercise (for readers to attempt at the end of this topic followed by a group discussion):

■ For each of the Cs, come up with a sample communication.

■ The first two Cs are completeness and conciseness. Do you think they are contradicting the core principle? Come up with your conclusion and justify the answer.

■ Which *C* according to you is most important in the list? Justify your choice.

■ Can you think of any other qualities that your communication must possess to make it effective?

Types of communication

Throughout this book, we will be looking at a range of types of communication. If you want your team to become top-notch communicators you want them to be adept at all forms of communication. Here are some key types of communication that is used on a regular basis to communicate with your peers, subordinates, managers, and customers. You perhaps may not have known that you used these many types of communication in your day-to-day communication. You will become acquainted with it over the course of this book.

Verbal communication needs nonverbal methods to enhance the effectiveness of the message it conveys. Nonverbal forms add context, perspective, and give life to what words cannot express. It is a fact that all of us use nonverbal forms more than words. The following diagram shows the different types of communication:

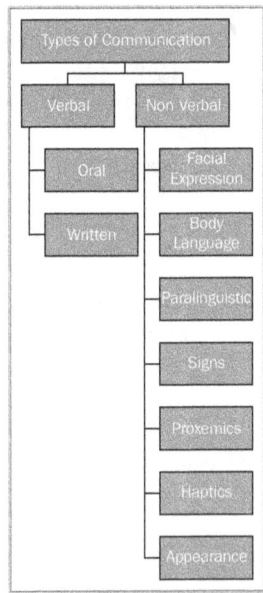

Let us look a little deeper into verbal and nonverbal forms of communication:

> **Oral communication**: Oral communication happens through voice waves. It includes telephonic talks, face-to-face discussions, and speeches in seminars, radio, TV, movies, and VOIP.

> **Written communication**: Any words written on paper, blogs, journals, and other mediums form written communication. Grammar, writing style, and vocabulary among others influence the quality it carries.

> **Facial expression**: Emotions are displayed on your face in contrast to the words that come out of your mouth. For nonbusiness matters, facial expression plays a crucial part in communicating the thoughts of the mind. In a business setting too, it can be leveraged in building partnerships, rapport, and win the interviewer over.

> **Body language**: Your body communicates, as much as the words do—or more. A hunched back, for example, suggests low confidence and crossed arms are a defensive posture. Body language can infect the entire atmosphere around you—don't let your moods dictate your body language, let positive body language brighten your mood.

> **Paralinguistic**: Paralinguistic is about the tone of your voice. This matters almost as much as the words themselves. Try shouting in a board meeting and you will see the ill effect of not controlling the paralinguistic.

> **Signs**: You come across signs every single day. Starting from your spouse showing a thumbs-up as a sign of approval for the breakfast you cooked, to the road signs you see indicating road bumps. They are a quick and easy way to communicate. Imagine if you had to read a paragraph to understand that the lane that you are traveling is merging with another in the next five hundred meters when you are traveling at 100 mph. Emoticons you use online or by text are good examples of signs that have crossed over into our lexicon.

> **Proxemics**: Proxemics refers to the spaces involved in communication. In face-to-face interaction, you need to have a certain distance between you and the listener. The distance is subjective and depends on a number of factors that influence you—like your culture, familiarity with the crowd, the situation, and your personality. If you want to communicate a secret to a near and dear one, you don't want to stand too far apart, do you?

> **Haptics**: Haptics deals with the science of touch. It is normal for humans to touch each other when we communicate. However, there are acceptable touches and those that aren't. You wouldn't want to be kissed in a business meeting but at home it is perfectly fine. In a business setting, handshake sounds preferable and needed between parties who trust each other but family members may hug to show affection.

> **Appearance**: What does personal appearance have to do with communication? Everything! Imagine having to listen to a disheveled manager about power dressing. Would it have the same effect if he had dressed aptly for a business setting? People in the corporate world must take extra care to ensure that they look sharp and dress to the occasion.

Action Point

Exercise (for readers to attempt at the end of this topic followed by a group discussion):

- Conduct a role play between a speaker and a listener. In the first instalment, let the speaker talk normally. And, the second time, let the speaker curtail face expressions, body movement, and intonations. Ask the listener to provide feedback on the two different experiences of communication.
- As a group, discuss how each individual feels about the physical distance maintained by others when communicating and the likes and dislikes of communicators who touch during the course of the conversation.
- What are some of the common signs you use on a daily basis and how does it feel to be signed by others?
- Do you discriminate in judging communicators by the way they look?

Different communication styles

Every individual is different and unique in their own way. Likewise, the way they communicate is different (if not unique) as well. The trick is to retain your own individual style, but not to allow this to compromise the quality of your communication. When training your employees, you need to give them the confidence to develop their own communicative style and to do so using a framework that sets quality and effectiveness above all else. On the other hand, it is also essential to understand the communication style of your interlocutor as well, as this will help you in responding and working with them.

Research has been ongoing since the early forties to study the various personalities that lead to different communication styles. William Marston, a psychologist, came out with a tool called as DISC, which broadly classified people into four distinct types:

> Dominance

> Influence

> Steadiness

> Compliance

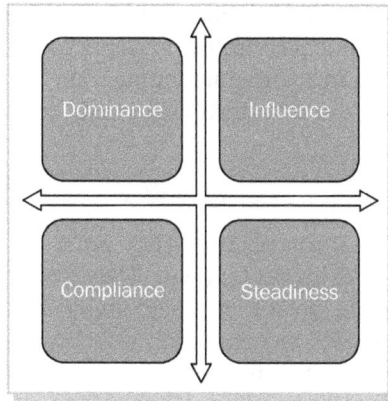

Every one of us falls in either one of these four personality groups and it is also possible that we have (cherry) picked from different groups. For communication to be effective, it is imperative that you understand the personality of your recipient and adjust your style to suit theirs. This is a disadvantage that all public speakers face when encountered with people who comes from all quadrants of life. In the next section, I will discuss each of the personalities and how you are expected to communicate with them. The only assumption I make here is that you are able to identify the right type.

Dominance

Dominance personalities are goal-oriented. Their target is towards the goal, and not the intricate details that take them towards it. They rely on facts, figures, and things on hand, and not necessarily the processes and procedures to accomplish their target. They are able to relate a number of distinct events and create a pattern. Problem solving comes naturally and so do creative ideas. On the downside, organization and people management skills may not be their strong set.

If you are communicating with a customer who has dominance style of communication, make sure that you talk about the things you achieved and leave out the methods you employed to achieve them, unless they ask for it. In IT especially, do not explain to customers or users (and even managers) how you achieved the objective unless specifically requested.

Influence

Influencers are people-oriented. They love the company of others, and center themselves in groups. They are the life of the party and derive their energy from others. They are easily distracted and can get bored if the conversation on a topic goes on for longer periods of time. Influencers are curious chaps and they are interested in sharing and getting updates from others. They can be highly expressive and are not afraid to talk their minds freely.

Influencers work well in teams. If you are managing influencers, be sure to place them in teams rather than in an individual contributor role. If you are talking to influencers, allow space for small talk, even in a corporate setting. Forget that it is all official in the workplace. Give them the freedom to express with words, to get the best out of them.

Steadiness

IT folk make excellent individual contributors. They can work in their own caves and come out with all the targets that are set for them. They would prefer to talk to you one-on one rather than in a group. They prefer to read and understand rather than sit in meetings and listen in. Even when they sit in meetings, they take in data mainly through their notes and minutes from meetings. They may not be the people who will make major decisions in a snap; instead, they might ask a lot of questions to be certain of the decision they make. In organizations, the steady kind make excellent conflict managers. Be sure to use them when conflicts arise.

Steadiness kind are opposite to Influencers. They love solitude and prefer to take time off from groups and self-reflect on what's happening and their thoughts. They draw their energy from within rather than people. They are steady, well balanced, and patient.

Compliance

Compliance personalities are like detectives. They take in data, facts, figures, and evidence among others to come out with their decision. They do not work on hunches like the dominant types. They take tried and tested methods and are not the adventurous kind. They may be more apt for running a business rather than transforming it.

In IT, things can go wrong. When something goes wrong, the root cause of the problem is not always known. If the cause is not known, it is a challenge to fix it. In this situation, you need people who can get their hands dirty by picking at everything they can lay their hands on. They deep dive into extracting system logs, questioning whoever is involved, and do whatever is necessary to solve the problem on hand. They are the compliance kind. They don't communicate with arbitrary facts and ballpark figures. They are all about factual accurate data. When you communicate with them, don't go empty-handed, provide them all the information you have and they will put things together. And be prepared to be asked a number of questions.

Action Point

Exercise (for readers to attempt at the end of this topic followed by a group discussion):

■ Identify your communication style by jotting down how you want to be communicated with and how different people communicate with you generally.

■ List down two people in your friends, family, and professional circles with each of the communication styles. Recollect how you communicated with them earlier and write down how you are going to communicate going forward.

Cross-cultural communication

The world is getting flatter by the day. People from different countries, culture, and color are staying in the same neighborhood, working in adjoining cubicles, and are dining out at the same joints. There is no more the crevice that puts barriers between people. This is one of the greatest gifts of the information age.

Yet, communication between different cultures is a tricky subject. Every culture has different set of practices, values, and meanings to certain words, gestures, and body movements. Before we talk about the divide between various cultures, I must share about the cultural difference between one IT organization to another. I was working as a consultant in a German corporation. In the present world, I found it somewhat amiss to find that employees in this organization addressed each other by *Mr.* and *Ms.* followed by their last name or in some cases first name and last name. And when e-mailing, it was always *Hello* and *Dear.* Throughout my career, I had never seen IT employees refer to each other this way. It has always been *Hi* and then the first name. For me, it took some getting used to with employees of this German organization. The employees of this organization hailed from the same city as I did, and yet, the differences loomed large. Imagine how the real cultural differences between one set of people with another would put things out in the open glaringly.

If you are visiting a different culture, remember the proverb *"Be a Roman in Rome".* You need to be flexible and adapt to the foreign culture. Every culture is different. For example, greeting each other with a peck is OK in France but in India, people either shake hands or say *Hello* from a distance. This is just one example, but I could probably write an entire book on cultural differences!

Differences in communication between cultures are a common occurrence. To ensure that the differences are minimal at best, and to be certain that effectiveness of communication is not hampered, make it a habit not to judge the messages you receive from people belonging to other cultures. Take a step back, pull in some fresh air, and think clearly on the underlying meaning. Confirm that you understood the message and then respond. Most communication issues happen due to confusion in language and misunderstanding the crux. Remember that the same words and similar phrases may mean different things in different countries.

When you are communicating with a person of a different culture like your customers, users, or peers, there are a number of things that you need to take care of. A few are listed here:

➤ When you speak to people from a different culture, speak slowly, and pronounce every syllable and every word properly.

➤ Do not use slang. People from other cultures may not understand your slang words.

➤ Do not use idioms and sayings with people from different cultures.

➤ You may be a humorous person but if the party listening in does not understand it, your talent will be awash with quizzical looks. Don't show off your humor.

➤ If you have a question to ask, ask one question at a time. A non-English speaker might find it difficult to answer all three questions concurrently.

Some cultures are direct in communication, while others are not. You need to understand the people you are dealing with. For example, people from Netherlands are direct communicators. They say yes or no to your face unlike my culture where we beat around the bush until there isn't any more bush to go about.

Like the words, your body language and gestures matter as well. Understand what to gesture and when to gesture. A thumbs-up sign generally means good job, but not in Australia and Greece. In these parts of the world, it simply implies "up yours".

The main thing is to simply be aware of those around you, their sensitivities, their beliefs, cultural norms, and expectations. While this is particularly true in a globalized world, in truth it is key for great communication in general.

Action Point

Exercise (for readers to attempt at the end of this topic followed by a group discussion):

■ Based on real-life examples, identify the differences (words and style of delivery) you find in communicators who are from a different culture than you. For example, an American will say "put it on the table" and an Indian could say "keep it on the table".

■ As a group, make a list of your out-of-culture contacts, and study their culture and communication style. Come out with a list of do's and don'ts when you communicate with them.

Rapport and relationship for effective communication

Couples who are in good harmonious relationships are comfortable around each other. They share everything, including the most trivial and deadly details of their lives. The rapport they share is the underlying cause for effective communication. Applying this thought to companies, employees must look for building rapport with fellow employees, customers, and vendors to improve communication between them.

Some people have an innate talent to make friends and build rapport within a matter of minutes, whereas others might not find it easy. I don't believe that rapport building is a natural talent alone; anybody can cultivate it and work at getting better at it. Throughout the process of training your employees, this notion of rapport building should remain important—if someone is able to build rapport effectively with others, they will easily be able to communicate. If you get your team building a healthy rapport with those around them, your job will be a lot easier!

I know a HR manager who makes it a point to walk around the office in the morning, visiting every nook and corner, exchanging pleasantries with key people in the organization. This genuine effort that the HR manager puts in has given her the edge to build rapport with employees in the organization. She has gone the extra mile (literally too) and has reaped the benefits that come of it.

In the coming chapters, I will provide a few pointers that you can use to build rapport with fellow employees. Remember that effective communication is possible only through healthy relationships, and relationships are made of rapport in every fiber. The objective of this workshop is to make communication effective, and developing rapport is one of the key building blocks.

Action Point

Exercise (for readers to attempt at the end of this topic followed by a group discussion):

- Have you experienced better communication through good relationships? Give examples that are not personal in nature.
- Observe yourself communicating with someone who you have a good rapport with and relatively a stranger who you meet a few days back. Share the differences between the two sets of communication experiences.

Summary

In this chapter, we have moved from the official policies and processes that govern communication in an organization, to the individual skills that are integral for communication in everyday scenarios. They may seem like completely separate things, but in the workplace they are closely related.

As this chapter ends, you should have an understanding of the following:

➤ Organizational hierarchy based on the pyramid and how communication binds them together

➤ The term governance and its importance in organizations

➤ The policy document and what it consists of

➤ The relationship between a policy and a process

➤ An understanding of a process and its applicability in communication

➤ The importance of the feedback mechanism

- ➤ 7 Cs of communication:
  - ➤ Completeness
  - ➤ Conciseness
  - ➤ Consideration
  - ➤ Concreteness
  - ➤ Courtesy
  - ➤ Clearness
  - ➤ Correctness

- ➤ Various types of communication:
  - ➤ Verbal
  - ➤ Nonverbal

- ➤ Communication styles:
  - ➤ Dominance
  - ➤ Influence
  - ➤ Steadiness
  - ➤ Compliance

- ➤ The need for rapport and relationships for building effective communication channels

In the next chapter, we will look at written communication and its various flavors—e-mails, mailers, notifications, visuals, infographics, and process maps. We will also discuss the common issues that crop up in written communication and the remedies for avoiding it.

>3
Written Communication

The emergence of the information age has made all of us writers. We cannot think of any form of communication that works without putting words together on paper or a word processor. It is ironic that the development of modern technology has actually returned us to one of the most traditional forms of communication. The way you write reflects your personality and the kind of individual you are.

Writing skills are essential at all levels in organizations. Most commonly used are e-mails, where everyday communication with peers, customers, and vendors are likely to come under scrutiny. And then there is the informal communication through instant messaging. Although it is not recognized as an official medium, words stated on instant messaging can always be used in more formal and official mediums. Documentation has become an essential part of professional life. Whatever your role, you are likely to be expected to prepare documents on a range of issues. A person who is adept at writing in any context will be looked upon favorably, but most importantly, it will help them perform their job effectively and easily. What are some of the objectives that written communication tries to accomplish in offices? If we start answering this question, how we do what we do can be decoded with ease. Here are a few universal pointers that you will learn in this chapter:

> ➤ Keep your writing succinct and to the point
> ➤ Follow the appropriate etiquette (such as e-mail etiquette) for all forms of communication
> ➤ Remember that most written forms of communication are admissible in court
> ➤ Written communication must reflect the values of the company
> ➤ Review the communication for subject matter, clarity, grammar, and spelling before you publish it
> ➤ Avoid displaying affection with peers or customers on official channels

Forms of written communication

E-mails, instant messaging, marketing material, blogs, documents, process maps, signs, and reports are various written mediums for communicating information. They convey one or more of the four forms of written communication that is used in the IT field on a day-to-day basis. Each form has its place, and every form is framed in such a way that it will communicate the required information and in the tone that the communication form demands.

While you discuss the individual forms of communication, to relate directly to the work performed in your organization, you can cite communication examples that fall under different forms.

Action-focused communication

In **action-focused communication**, the content is aimed at getting things done. The style is direct and the emphasis is on producing results. This form of communication must be used in an active voice to emphasize the actions to be performed, and the energy that propels this forward. Along with actions, it can be laced with a motivational style to produce the desired results.

An e-mail instructing the team to do certain activities is a good example of action-focused communication. **Minutes of meetings** (MoM) where actions are recorded and attributed to the responsible parties fits into this category very well. The medium can be e-mails, minutes, instant messaging, or visual posters, while the form should be instructive in nature and aim at keeping things in motion towards the target.

When you frame an action-focused communication, always keep in mind the following:

> ➤ In this form of communication, you have an objective to achieve, and the communication must sound like instructions in carrying out the objectives.

> ➤ It must be like a to-do list. Do this, do that. Don't do this and don't do that.

> ➤ Use everyday simple language and do not embellish the communication with fancy words.

> ➤ Every action-focused communication must have a designated owner and a target completion date set in the future.

> ➤ The target completion date cannot be something like ASAP or when a customer provides information.

Here's an example:

Action description	Responsibility	Deadline
Clean up active directory users to remove duplicate and dummy users	John Doe (use names and not roles)	Sep 25, 13
Test redundant switch's configuration and the auto failover mechanism	Jane Doe	Oct 30, 13

In the preceding example, the two action-focused communication samples are telling John and Jane Doe on the activities to complete and timeline as well.

Influential communication

When you try to influence a person or an organization towards a particular direction or decision, this form of written communication is classified under influential communication. Your focus is to convince, and to justify the actions that are to be taken. You need to appeal to your interlocutor in a way that gets them on your side. You can do this through the content of your communication, which should effectively offer them something, such as a specific reason to act in a certain way or do a specific task. However, you can also do this through this in the way it is delivered, addressing the other person or, indeed, group of people in a way that moves the reader in doing what is intended—not primarily by the power of your authority but through the supporting and justifications that you provide. Influential communication is used at all layers of the organization. A typical example could be an employee writing to his manager requesting for a change in role. He lists down the benefits that the organization would reap from moving him to the targeted role.

A business development manager creates proposals for new business opportunities. His intent is to show the value proposition to the customer by highlighting the value that the customer gets out of the business relationship and the various add-ons that come with the service. He might put in a few more angles of justification through cost-benefit analysis, case studies of what has been done earlier, and profiles of people running the organization, among others.

To write to influence, use the following tips and you should be in a better position to get things done in your preferred way:

> ➤ Identify what you would like to achieve through this communication. Be precise and clear not simply about what you want done, but, more importantly, why you want it done and what the benefits will be.

> ➤ If you want to influence someone, they need to understand what the benefits of listening to you will be. Use a conversational tone as the personal nature of the communication influences the reader to act in your favor; again, this is about appealing to the person or people you are communicating with.

➤ You need them to view you as working in everyone's interests. However, you must also keep in mind that you need to also communicate some sense of authority—you should, however, be able to achieve this through the first bullet point.

➤ Remember that the world does not run on charity, but purely on financials (especially in the business world!). So, a win-win situation should be presented to the reader. Through this communication, tell the reader what they would get by acting out your wishes, and how it would be beneficial—for them, the team, or the organization.

In the following example, I have applied the tips that I have shared with you. As you can read in the example, the soft skill coach has an objective he wants to achieve, and he is aiming for it by convincing the learning and development manager that he is right man for the job. This type of communication is a big field of study by itself. People have different ways of influencing other people. Imagination and creativity is key in exceling in influential communication.

The following example is an e-mail from a soft skill coach to a learning and development manager in an IT organization:

Hello Mr. John Doe,

Thank you for contacting me on my website. I am glad you have gone through the website, the services that I can offer, and my profile as a soft skill coach. I have been coaching corporates and students on soft skills for the past 22 years and I have penned several books pertaining to the topics I coach.

(Note here how the writer establishes themselves as a figure of authority, as if to underline to the reader that they are worth listening to.)

From your e-mail, I understand that you are looking to reduce the conflicts between team members of the IT department and with other employees in the organization.

(Here the writer is acknowledging "John Doe's" problem—the writer's words here act in a way that says "I understand your problem".)

I want to assure you that you have sought the perfect person to mitigate the issue that you are facing in your organization. From the limited information you have provided, it seems to be that the conflicts are due to lack of understanding and effective communication.

(Again, you can see that the writer is establishing themselves as an authority, someone to be trusted.)

This is common in most organizations. I have designed training and workshop sessions to address these issues in organizations. After going through the sessions, organizations are reaping benefits of improved communication, increased productivity, and reduced tautness. I can provide you with references along with the financial information in my next communication.

Do let me know if you want to take our discussion forward and forge a new business relationship.

(The writer closes here in a way that is both amicable and personable while also being all about business; this demonstrates professionalism and suggests mutual benefits, while also presenting yourself as someone that the reader will want to work with on a personal level.)

Thanks,

John Smith

Trainer and Coach

Negative communication

We have looked at two forms of communication in action-focused and influential communications that toe the positive line. The opposing one—negative communication—plays its part in the world of communication as well. This form of communication passes on information that will not bring cheer to the recipient. This style must not beat around the bush or give the history and geography of the subject before coming to the crux of the matter. It must be as direct as possible and aimed at closing the communication channel as soon as possible. But, it must contain essences of empathy to alleviate the pain that this form of communication is known to transfer.

Negative communication is used by all employees in an organization and at all levels of the business. A warning letter shot out to erring employees or a companywide layoff to unfortunate employees are some examples at a people management level. In the business world, termination of a contract or penalty imposed communication are some popular examples.

When you are writing negative communication, keep the following principles in mind:

> ➤ Don't beat around the bush. Be straightforward and put it out as plainly as you can.

> ➤ Justify the reasons why you are sending out the negative type of written communication.

> ➤ What next? Just sending out a negative message is not enough. You need to tell the recipient what the result of this communication is, whether it's a warning as per the following example, or loss of contract, and so on.

The following example is a warning e-mail sent by the human resources manager to an erring employee:

> *Hi Jane Doe,*
>
> *It has come to our notice that you are smoking on the office premises although we have put up signs clearly indicating that smoking is prohibited within the campus. Your act has brought disrepute to our organization and will potentially attract penalties from the government.*
>
> *We would like to warn you that a similar offence hereafter will be dealt with severely. Treat this letter as the last and final warning.*
>
> *Let me know if you have any further questions regarding the content of this letter.*
>
> *Thanks,*
>
> *John Doe*
>
> *HR Manager*

Communicating information

The last type of communication that is widely used is informational communication. As the name suggests, this type of communication conveys information—nothing more, nothing less. This type of communication works best if it is succinct and clear. Abstractness and dramatics are to be avoided in this type of communication. Also, it is important that the information communicator preempts all possible questions from the recipients and answers the questions in it.

Information communication is used across all layers of the organization. Some examples include a frequently asked questions section, a memo about organizational changes, and status updates from vendors and peers.

When drafting this type of communication, keep the following tips in mind:

> ➤ Do not use a personalized message as you do in influential communication. It is written for the third party and must be far from all emotions. It must exactly read like a news report, which aims at providing unbiased information.
>
> ➤ Information must be as terse as possible. Once again, complicated words do not convey information effectively and can confuse the meaning of it.
>
> ➤ Do not be abstract. The message must be straightforward.

Action Point

Exercise (for readers to attempt at the end of this topic followed by a group discussion):

- Create a list of action points from your project, against the timelines and the person responsible for performing the activity. Discuss action points with the class to see if they adhere to the rules of action-focused communication.
- Write an e-mail to your manager asking for a pay rise with credible justifications.
- List down various circumstances in your organization when negative communication has been used. Compare the nature with the pointers provided in this chapter.
- According to you, what is the best channel to communicate information to employees—from your manager and from the higher management? State reasons for the chosen communication channel.

Jargon

IT teams work primarily on hardcore technical subjects. They get immersed in their respective fields, and the terminologies used on the job will become second nature and get added to their overall vocabulary. When an employee communicates, the words acquired from their field of work are used freely, and differentiating work-related terminologies with normal speech will be like picking out a needle in a haystack. The employee may not be aware that certain words used are not understood by people outside the profession. This is referred to as jargon. In other words, jargon is a form of technical terminology and it can be highly subjective in nature. What may seem like everyday language to you may be impenetrable to someone else.

Jargon, although often irritating, can be useful when used in the right context. It provides a short form of expressing difficult ideas. The problem is that IT folks may not necessarily know when to use it and when not to. Jargon innocently used without considering the target audience could come across as arrogant and insincere in the eyes of the beholder. Some use jargon as a way of impressing others, but it can rarely be pulled off; rather, it leaves a bad impression.

Here are some tips to help IT employees know how to handle jargon:

- Be aware of when to use jargon. Jargon is sometimes necessary but is best avoided during most communication.
- Start by identifying the recipient of communication. The intended target audience could be peers within the team or a customer.
- Gauge the subject knowledge that the recipient could possess. There is no prescribed way to do it, go by instinct. When communicating with customers, avoid jargon usage by default. When communicating with a peer, jargon may be useful as it shortens the message and increases the effectiveness.

> ➤ Get the communication reviewed by somebody outside the subject matter when messaging customers, or anybody outside the technical team.

> ➤ Employ tools such as MS Word that fail to recognize certain terminologies. When the wavy red lines appear, it is an indication of words that are outside the ambit of normal English words.

> ➤ Default communication must be simple everyday language. Alternately, a style guide can be prepared and circulated to the team.

Action Point

Exercise (for readers to attempt at the end of this topic followed by a group discussion):

- Identify the jargon that you use on a regular basis. Also, against each instance of jargon, put a check mark indicating whether the word has gone into the communication involving the customer (or somebody outside the technical team).

- What are some of the communication mediums in your organization that justify the use of jargon? Hint: contract documents, technical guides, and so on.

- List the jargon that the customer uses and start employing them in your mutual communication.

- Identify a technical situation at work. Communicate the situation with peers in a language that is understood by peers (read with jargon). Now, the second part of the exercise is to convey the same information to the customer. How can you explain it without recourse to jargon?

Project updates

In IT, unlike other industries where there are separate teams to convey information, most employees communicate on a regular basis—either with customers or vendors, and definitely between peers and other parts of the organization. The preferred medium is through e-mails if there isn't a sense of urgency and when formal communication is to be made. For urgent and informal information exchanges, an instant messaging engine is generally used. Apart from these, IT teams employ portals and ticketing systems to store knowledge, track activities and convey real-time updates to customers and stakeholders. It might sound simple enough, but it isn't. There are numerous cases of wrong interpretation by customers and conflicts within teams as project updates were not communicated the right way and through the proper channels. In this section, we will touch base upon communicating project- or job-specific updates between peers and to customers.

Peer-to-peer communication

Peer-to-peer communication must be effective to ensure that teamwork is realized in delivering the best results to customers. Remember that your peers are from the same organization and if there is any information about the customer, or technical tips, it must be shared freely. When you are communicating with each other, lay out everything as it happened, and do not hide any information from one another. Open and hurdle-free communication is the base upon which you can achieve project-related goals. Be honest to one another, and when you communicate state the facts in their entirety.

Communication among peers is generally informal. If the communication is between one-on-one, choose a medium such as instant messaging, which is perhaps the fastest and easiest way to communicate through written words. If you need to address a larger group, and would like to keep this communication documented for the future, go for an e-mail.

In a nutshell, here is what you should do while communicating with peers:

> ➤ Do not hide anything with peers regarding job-related activities. State the facts, as it happened and to the tee.

> ➤ Employ simple and straightforward language.

> ➤ State your suppositions as your personal opinion and not based on facts. The principle is to clearly demarcate facts from opinions, biases, and theories.

> ➤ Get answers immediately with instant messaging systems. If the information sought can wait and is formal in nature, opt for e-mails. For example, if the support teams require a customer's concurrence to restart a server, they will contact the customer, either through instant messaging or a telephone and obtain approval. They will follow it up with an e-mail, requesting formal approval.

Let me illustrate further with an example. During a routine maintenance activity, Technician A changes the configuration of a server, mistaking it for another server in the same data center. This results in an outage of the e-mail service. Technician B receives the complaint from the customer regarding the outage identifies the fault and fixes the issue. Upon checking the logs, Technician B identifies the error committed by Technician A. Technician B is supposed to report the matter to his manager and provide an outage report to the customer. How will this be done?

When communicating with his manager, Technician B is expected to communicate the facts as they happened. State the facts as they were seen, preferably with a timeline and leaving out judgmental thoughts that would have resulted from the blunder.

It could look something like this:

> *00:06 – Received call from customer regarding e-mail outage*
>
> *00:10 – Logged the ticket in the system*
>
> *00:14 – Initial diagnosis of the server revealed that configuration was wrong*
>
> *00:17 – Modified configuration, which rectified the issue*
>
> *00:22 – Studied the logs, configuration was changed with Technician A's login*
>
> *00:35 – Checked with Technician A, and the configuration change was supposedly for a maintenance server, Technician A regrets messing up with the wrong server*

Customer communication

While honesty and integrity are integral parts of all communication, especially with customers, there is a limit as to how much you can communicate with the customer; it is generally advisable not to air dirty linen in public. The customer is entitled to know the status of the project and the reason for outage, but he doesn't need to know the finer details. Give the customer 20,000 feet description—high level status updates that are truthful and useful to the customer. An update such as *project is progressing* is not helpful to the customer but something specific such as *completed testing payment cart integration* is helpful.

Communication with customers is mostly formal. E-mail is the best medium to communicate with customers. In some cases, customers are also linked through instant messaging, and can seek out updates on the chat tool. Use the instant messaging tool to provide updates on an ad hoc basis only, and e-mails are a must for all regular updates. Do not substitute an e-mail with any other form. Especially with customers, you need documented proof of the targets achieved.

Here is what you need to do when you communicate with the customer:

> ➤ Between your customer and you, everything is bound by a contract. Remember that nothing is informal between the two of you.
>
> ➤ When you provide information to customer, do it in such a way that it is objective and not subjective. For example, tell the customer why their server went down. Don't tell them which engineer was responsible for the outage and all the stories that follow.
>
> ➤ Do inform customers with integrity. Don't distort facts. It will come back to bite you in the bottom. Yet, knowingly, many organizations twist the facts and present a bad case as an everyday affair.
>
> ➤ Insist on a customer sending you e-mails for carrying out activities. A verbal nod or approval should not be accepted.
>
> ➤ Some customers might connect with you on instant messaging, and there isn't anything wrong with chatting with them. But, be sure to ask for a mail when decisions are made by the customer.

For the same scenario that I illustrated earlier, here's is a sample e-mail communication sent to a customer. Observe that the facts are neither distorted nor twisted. Details pertaining to the technician involved are withheld:

Hi Steve,

Please find the details of the outage below.

Outage Summary: E-mail service was inaccessible between 00:06 and 00:17.

Outage Duration: 11 minutes.

Reason for Outage: Error in configuration caused the e-mail service to go down.

Resolution Applied: Configuration was rectified to resolve the issue.

Do let us know if you have further questions.

Thanks,

Jane Doe

This high-level update where you state the necessary details is good for any outside the organization such as vendors, suppliers, and the government. If somebody is not a part of the organization, maintain a rule of thumb not to share all the information, just state high-level facts and leave it at that.

It is likely that your customers would not come back to you asking more questions as long as the objective is getting achieved. If they do, you can probably go one step ahead and mention that human error was the cause of the outage, but in no case reveal who is behind the damage.

The real reason why I am providing you with this example is that when we e-mail or talk to our customers, we need to stay above board of organizational politics, team performance, and internal squabbles. Respond to a customer as though your organization is one single unit and the blame, if any, is on the entire organization but not on any individual teams or individuals. I am aware that I am repeating myself here but there is a reason to do this. Telling customers everything is an epidemic that is plaguing the IT industry today. This gives customers an undue advantage in negotiations and abiding by the contract.

E-mails

Today, e-mail is the most common form of communication. This form is attractive due to their remote nature. Not only that, but it is also a form of communication that is not bound by specific etiquette—it can be used formally or informally. With popularity comes greater responsibility. The content of the e-mail must be as perfect as it can get. E-mails are admissible in courts in most parts of the world, so it makes perfect sense to get the e-mailing part right, every time. If you are on a call and say something inappropriate, you can always apologize and say that you were distracted for a moment or you weren't thinking else you can also claim that you never said anything like it. You cannot claim the same with the e-mail. The proof is in the words, and it cannot be altered. What you put on an e-mail will hold you to it as long as you are liable.

In IT, e-mails play a major role in exchanging information. Hence, it is imperative that IT employees are equipped with etiquette that allows them to effectively and efficiently communicate. All IT employees must understand that e-mails are powerful if used correctly and can be deadly if they screw up. A correctly worded e-mail can do wonders in building the confidence of customers and stakeholders and on the flipside, it can make the same parties wonder about the capabilities of the IT organization. Remember that customers judge the organization by the way you communicate, and to reiterate, communication in IT happens mainly through e-mails.

E-mail policy

E-mail communication is an integral part of any organization. Governing the use of e-mail is an essential act to safeguard the company's reputation. It also brings in the discipline that provides the boundaries for employees to work within. An e-mail policy should be in place not to restrict the usage of e-mails, but to ensure that it is used for the right purpose. In this section, I want to emphasize the importance of e-mail policies and would like to inform the trainees that policies are in place to safeguard the communication boundaries and to protect the organization, the team, and the employee from getting into a difficult positions.

The sample provided in this section could be the starter pack to get you started on developing an e-mail policy for your organization.

E-mail etiquette

In a corporate setting, there is e-mail etiquette that is considered necessary by the community. In this section, I am giving you a basic list of e-mail etiquette that will help you improve communication, minimize tension, and standardize the activity surrounding e-mails. This list is by no means comprehensive. Add further to it depending on your organization and its policies. Once the list is finalized, I would recommend that the list be printed out and pinned on every workstation for a few weeks. Seeing the etiquette constantly, breeds familiarity and the subconscious mind starts to follow the etiquette unknowingly. Here's a basic list of e-mail etiquette:

> Always start the e-mail draft by addressing the recipient with a *Hi* or *Dear* and end with a thanking note—a simple thanks followed by your name.

> Review the e-mail content and your recipient list before sending out the e-mail.

> Always insert the summary of the e-mail in the subject line.

> Do not use CAPS, either in the body of the e-mail or in the subject line. It is not appropriate in a professional setting. In fact, it is considered rude outside professional circles as well.

> Do not hit reply all unless you are absolutely sure that everyone in the mail chain is to be updated with your message. Especially when you want to thank someone, send the e-mail to the specific person only.

> I discussed conciseness in the 7 Cs of communication. Be sure to apply it here. E-mails are meant to be to the point, and direct. Do not beat around the bush and elongate them.

- ➤ If you are sending attachments, mention it in the e-mail specifying the exact contents.

- ➤ All e-mails must carry a signature indicating your name, designation, and your coordinates.

- ➤ If you are forwarding e-mails, let the recipients know what they are supposed to do with it. Just don't hit the forward button and leave it at that. Add an FYI at least. It tells the recipient that there is no action to be taken; rather, it's information to be digested.

- ➤ When you are out of office during business hours, use an auto responder to let people know that there will be a delay in response.

- ➤ Run a spell and grammar check before hitting SEND.

- ➤ When you are in an angry, don't send out any e-mails. Your emotions are reflected in the content, and it is bound to have undesirable effects.

- ➤ Acknowledge all e-mails addressed to you.

Action Point

Exercise (for readers to attempt at the end of this topic followed by a group discussion):

- ■ You are on a vacation and you did not inform your customers. Your customers e-mail you and when they don't get a response within a day or two, they escalate the matter to your manager only to find out that you are on vacation. How could you have avoided this escalation and improved on customer experience?

- ■ You sent out an e-mail to prospective vendors regarding a service that you would like to obtain. One of the vendors was not clear on your requirements and wanted to talk to you to sort out the shortcoming. How and where would he find your contact information in the e-mail?

- ■ Employ the etiquette as mentioned in this section. E-mail etiquette is designed to bring a professional look to e-mails and standardize how employees communicate. Pick out random e-mails to be shared with the group and review them against the etiquette.

- ■ Provide two examples of when you would avoid sending out an e-mail; instead employ one of the other forms of communication. What are the reasons for not sending out an e-mail and why did you choose a particular form of communication in its place?

E-mail templates

When IT teams are sending out status updates, reports, and other repetitive e-mails, employing e-mail templates brings in the much needed standardization to the communication activity. We wouldn't want to go to the extent of creating templates for ad hoc e-mails such as responding to a customer's query and asking one of the vendors to pull up their socks. Use templates only for e-mail communications that are scheduled, repetitive, and those that do not necessarily request a response.

In the following sample template, I have considered a weekly report that goes out to the customer. This template would be essentially saved in a Microsoft Word document. And, the employee scheduled to send out status update e-mail must insert relevant information in place of <…> and send the e-mail. The beauty of such templates is that every week, the format, the fonts, and the style of reporting will stay constant. And the customer knows exactly where to look for in the e-mail for specific information of interest.

Hi <customer's first name>,

For the week ending <week ending date>, please find the number of assets discovered on the network. The asset inventory has been updated with these numbers.

Asset Details	Number of Assets Discovered
Servers	<number of servers discovered>
Switches	<number of switches discovered>
SAN/NAS	<number of SAN/NAS discovered>
Routers	<number of routers discovered>

Do write to asset.team@myorganization.com if you require clarifications on these numbers.

Thank you,

<Your name>

Asset Coordinator

Ph.: <Your number>

My Organization

Depending on the e-mail program the organization leverages, the template creation procedure can vary. But, there is a workaround to standardize it too:

➤ Employ Microsoft Word as your base for creating e-mail templates. Select the font you would like to use, spacing, font color, and other style elements.

➤ In the template, at places where you need to add specific information pertaining to an e-mail, indicate by with the help of < and > sign, which means that this section needs to be populated with relevant information before sending out the e-mail. Refer to my sample template to see how it is used.

➤ To add tables, I generally use Microsoft Excel separately and then import it to Word from the Excel application. There are inbuilt tables within Word but I have experienced that it is a lot easier working with Excel rather than Word. To import, I know you are going to shoot me for putting it here; it is just a copy and paste action.

> ➤ Likewise, if I need to use flowcharts or any other graphics, I employ Microsoft PowerPoint and import them over to Word.

> ➤ You can build signatures into the templates or it can be loaded onto the e-mail program such as Microsoft Outlook or IBM Lotus Notes. It works the same in both cases. The sample I have provided is typical of most IT organizations, which does not carry anything fancy.

> ➤ The e-mail template must be stored in a central storage area, and IT employees must be instructed to retrieve it from the central storage every time they send out an e-mail. This will ensure that if there are any changes done to the template, it can automatically reflect on all the e-mails going forward.

Here are a few generic pointers that I want you to consider before coming up with templates:

> ➤ Do not use fancy fonts. Fancy fonts are not considered professional. Examples include Comic Sans, Brush Script, and Impact among others.

> ➤ The fonts displayed on the recipient's e-mail are fetched from their system. If the employed font is unavailable, then the e-mail automatically switches to a default font, possibly altering the intended format and colors. To avoid this possible format logjam, use a font that is popular and widely used. Examples include Calibri, Book Antiqua, and Verdana among others.

> ➤ Always ask for feedback, and mention the channels through which the feedback can be given.

> ➤ Signatures across the organization must be built in the specified format. In some corporate circles, I have seen employees place humorous quotes below their signatures. It is not professional. Stay away from branding yourself with such quotes.

Visual communication

Visual communication is a form of written communication where ideas and information are conveyed through images, shapes, icons, and symbols. It is believed to be the oldest form of written communication as there is evidence to suggest that pre-historic man drew images of animals and rituals among others on cave walls and ceilings. The beauty of visual communication is that by itself, it is language and culture independent. You could practically use it in any part of the world, and you would be conveying the same set of ideas. If visual communication is amalgamated with words, the information that is conveyed becomes more powerful than either one form of communication can communicate on its own. In this workshop, we are going to look into the union on visual aids and words, and the outcome will be exchange of information and ideas quickly and effectively.

In an IT organization, you can typically use visual communication in a number of ways. The idea is to place visual aids in areas that matter, and not overdo it. These are like your trump cards that you utilize at the right place and at the right time. In this book so far, you have seen me use certain visual aids to illustrate certain ideas. I have used a two-dimensional cartoon for illustrating a breakdown in communication in projects, as the visual dimension of the image helps the understanding in a way that words cannot.

In this section, I will showcase a few scenarios where visual communication can be employed. And we will explore a few types of visual communication techniques that are most commonly employed in IT organizations. Remember that different situations demand different types of visual communication, the same type of visual set may not apply for all situations.

Flowcharts

Scenario 1: You are in a customer meeting for kick starting a new project for supporting PC hardware and software. The customer has shared the agenda stating that they are keen on understanding the process that our organization would employ in supporting them.

In this case, I have two options. I can tell the customer how the process works through the way of bullets, or show the customer how the process will flow visually. I will provide a demonstration of both. You can be the judge of what works best. Here are the two options:

➤ **Method 1: Bullets**

> ➤ Customer has a PC issue

> ➤ Customer calls the support number

> ➤ Level 1 technician logs a support ticket

> ➤ Level 1 technician diagnoses and resolves the issue

> ➤ If the level 1 technician is unable to resolve the problem, the issue is referred to level 2

> ➤ Level 2 technician troubleshoots and resolves the issue

> ➤ If level 1 has resolved the issue, then level 1 technician will take confirmation from customer

> ➤ If level 2 has resolved the issue, then level 1 technician will take confirmation from customer

> ➤ Support ticket is closed post- confirmation

➤ **Method 2: Flowchart**

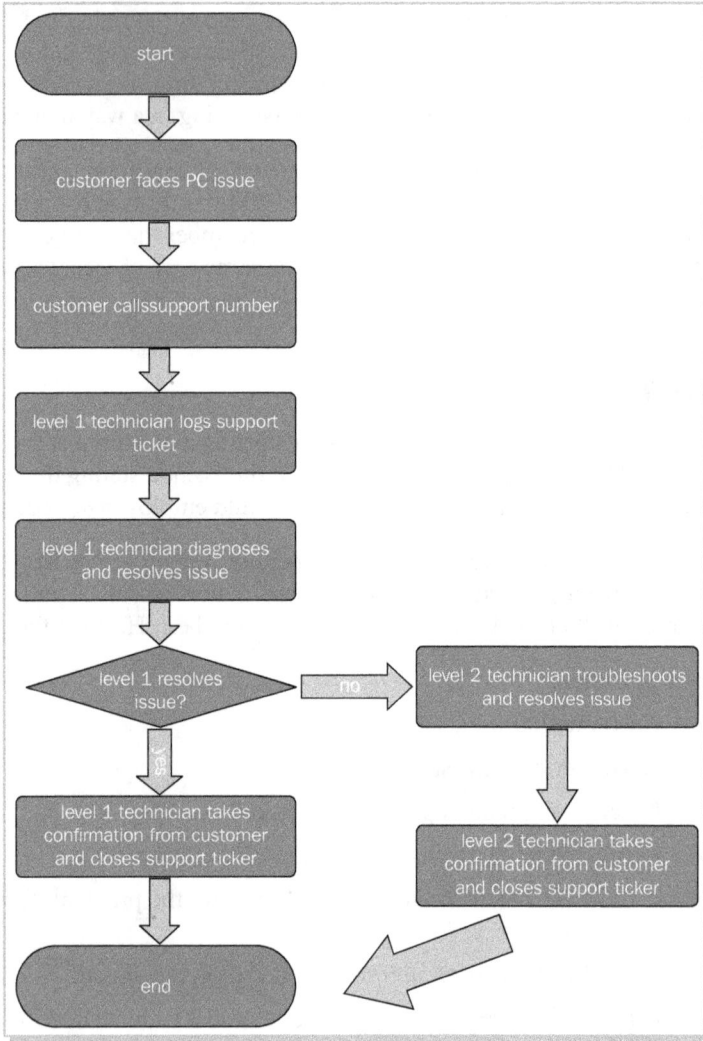

Analyzing the situation. To meet the requirements of *Scenario 1*, do you feel *method 1* is better suited than *method 2*. Definitely not. The visual appeal that flowcharts provide is unmatchable, no matter how many words you substitute for it. The audience can read and understand *method 2* easier than *method 1*, and the time needed to grasp is quicker too. Thereby, communication renders effective and efficient.

What are flowcharts?

Flowcharts are an integral part of an IT organization's communicative activities. Every objective to be achieved can be broken down into individual steps. Identifying the individual activities and integrating them together to bring out the bigger picture is the ideal way of going about it. The various individual activities and their relationships with one another can be illustrated effectively through a flowchart. Organizations involved in the development of software, the logic behind the coding can be effectively displayed using flowcharts. In projects that employ sequential design process, flowcharts are like gold. The workflow that I used in *Chapter 1, Communication Training*, to explain communication process is a type of flowchart.

I have provided another sample sequential flowchart that is widely used in IT organizations employing project management methodologies. This illustration is a mere example; you can apply it to any process, or any methodologies you follow. The community that this visual communication is directed towards understands the idea quickly and the image retains in their memory for a longer period—thereby rendering visual communication effective. The example given below is a 5-step waterfall model that is widely used in the software development industry.

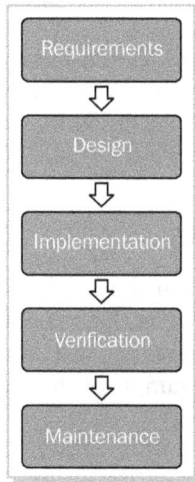

You can employ a sequential flowchart to communicate the detailed activities that you are going to perform for a customer. Flowcharting must be employed effectively, and here are some tips to create effective sequential flowcharts:

➤ Understand the individual activities before starting to draft a flowchart.

➤ Provide each individual activity with a recognizable name that is meaningful, which provides a basic understanding of what the activity is all about. In the sample flow chart, the individual activity names will point you in the direction of what could take place in the activity.

➤ Every individual activity has an input, output, and a trigger. Identify these and keep this documented. These may not necessarily go into the flowchart, but it is necessary for explaining the flowchart and training employees on it.

➤ You can further expand on this concept by tagging responsibilities for every activity. For example, in the sample, we could mention that the customer provides the requirements, the design team provides a solution, and the software team implements the solution and so on.

➤ I have indicated rectangle boxes only. But, there are a number of symbols that are employed, and each carry respective significance:

> Oval boxes indicate the start or the end of a process/activity.

> Rectangle boxes indicate individual activities as I have illustrated.

> If the activity involves taking decisions, use a decision box that is represented by a diamond box. For example, if the application throws an error, escalate to the coding team or deploy onto the server.

> Input and output to individual activities are represented by a parallelogram.

> The flow of activities from one to another is indicated with arrows.

Scenario 2: Continuing from scenario 1, the customer wants to know how the organization is structured. All customers ask for this information as they like to seek out the escalation paths and negotiate with decision makers rather than people lower down in the chain.

Hierarchical flowcharts

You can provide the information that customer has provided using bullets (textual) or employ hierarchical flowcharts that depict the hierarchical relationships. Take a look at the following sample organization chart and judge whether a customer would be happy to see the flow of information. Here's a sample of the hierarchical flowchart:

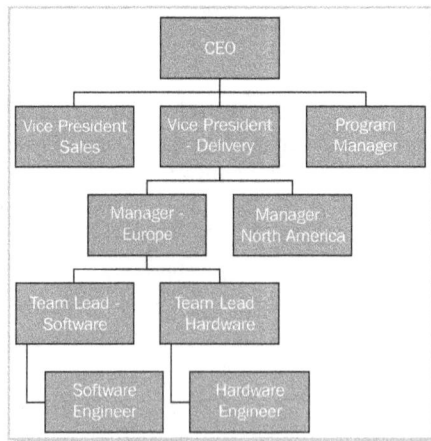

There are a number of types of flowcharts that you can employ. If you are using a software program such as Microsoft PowerPoint, it readily offers a number of flowcharts that you can readily use. I have created the flowcharts using the same software program as well. Remember that every type of flowchart can be used in a particular situation, so use it wisely and prudently.

Tables and graphs

Scenario 3: Another agenda in the customer meeting that you are in mentions a project that you are going to undertake. The customer wants to know the tentative schedule for the delivery of their project.

> **Method 1: Bullets**

>> Week 1 and 2: Source resources from product vendors

>> Week 1, 2, and 3: Interview candidates and bring them onboard

>> Week 2: Design architecture

>> Week 1 and 3: Discussions around the architecture and finalization

>> Week 4: Test procured products

>> Week 4 and 5: Implement architecture simulation and test

>> Week 6: Deploy architecture

>> Week 7: Test and close

> In this method, the customer gets a fair view of what is planned for which weeks. But, how easily can it be deciphered if the customer wants to know what is getting done in week 2? Let's try this out visually.

> **Method 2: Tables**

> Here is a visual layout of the same information that is offered in the earlier method:

Activities	Week 1	Week 2	Week 3	Week 4	Week 5	Week 6	Week 7
Source resources from product vendors	▓	▓					
Interview candidates and onboarding	▓	▓	▓				
Design architecture		▓					
Discussions around architecture and finalization	▓		▓				
Test procured products				▓			
Implement architecture simulation and test				▓	▓		
Deploy architecture						▓	
Test and close							▓

Green cells indicate the work being accomplished against the activity listed in the respective row. So, if a customer wants to see what is getting accomplished in *Week 3*, just look at the column under *Week 3*, and you get all that you need. It is decipherable easier than the text, and provides a holistic view of how things are shaping up.

The example that I provided is a fairly simple one. You can scale it up to any of the scheduling communications that you are in charge of.

What are tables?

Tables and graphs are a form of visual communication as well. They are extensively used in IT organizations mainly when numbers come into play.

The tables that I am referring to here are the arrangement of information into rows and columns. It is effective when comparing different sets of data. Placing data in tables enables you to analyze it easily, and come out with conclusions. When you are conveying information through tables, recipients can quickly grasp the message you are trying to pass, and thus rendering it effective. Here's an example of the sales figures in a year:

PC Sales Figures	
January	PCs sold
February	65321
March	70156
April	84548
May	50548
June	20158
July	33458
August	58785
September	55854
October	60258
November	70125
December	65558

You must necessarily employ tables when you are providing data that compares one set to the other—monthly numbers as indicated in the preceding sample. Placing data in tables is the ideal way to justify the analysis you have conducted and decisions that are taken. Remember that when you justify your action with figures, it pretty much seals the deal, and your decision will be accepted. Tables are numbers, and could be straining to the eye and confusing to the mind. To overcome these shortcomings, we can use charting techniques to bring in the visual appeal. Graphs are the quickest way to convince your stand and emphasize the point you are making. Also, it is perhaps the fastest way to communicate information. They are used primarily to indicate trends and display relationships between discrete sets of data.

They can be a particularly useful tool for analysis. One can trend future forecasts using graphs, and perform a variety of actions based on it. Here's a graph for the previous table. See how the communication gets enhanced and becomes effective in conveying the information that you wish to pass across.

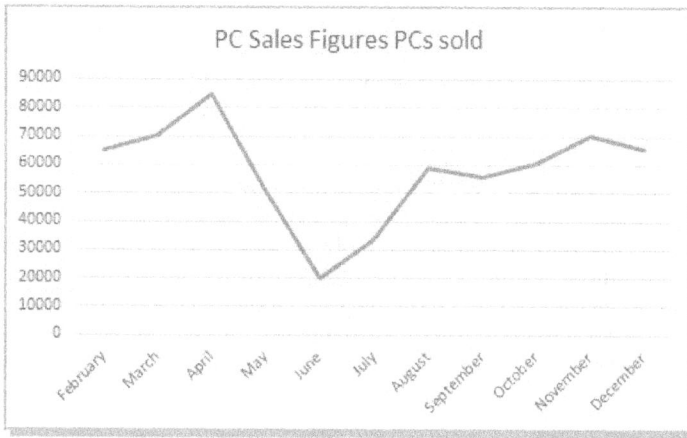

The recipient can decipher that the sales were good during the first quarter of the year, and the numbers started to dip in the second quarter. In the second half of the year, sales started to boom again. In the IT world, you can use graphs to highlight your performance to the customer, and highlight the achievement of your team to the senior management and with your team to showcase their achievements. Likewise, employees can employ tables and graphs to indicate a number of types of information that are based on numbers.

To play with numbers and charts, Microsoft Excel is the most apt tool. It is a tool that is most important to all organizations. If you haven't mastered it yet, you must do it sooner rather than later.

Imagination is key

In visual communication, imagination is everything. I have provided a couple of different ways of putting information across, and there are a number of other ways the same data could have been visualized.

As a general rule of thumb, any lists that are usually put under bullets, numbers that showcase the performance, and trends can be easily visualized under various forms. You need to put your head into the data you wish to share and the visualization just reveals itself to you. Also, as you gain experience in presenting data, you sync your thinking towards visualizing everything you see. Presentations must be peppered with visuals and that is the best way of enlivening the long hours you end up spending in the meeting room.

Action Point

Exercise (for readers to attempt at the end of this topic followed by a group discussion):

- You are a manager and you have 5 people in your team who have completed a project. You want to show visually the percentage of work each one of them has put in, in getting the project successfully completed. Person 1 has put in 10 percent, person 2-22 percent, person 3-54 percent, person 4-5 percent, and person 5-9 percent.

- Have you heard of SWOT analysis? It stands for strengths, weaknesses, opportunities, and threats. You can analyze almost everything using this analysis. I can analyze a subordinate in my team by stating the strengths the person possesses, their weaknesses, the opportunities that will launch the person to higher limits, and the weaknesses that drag the person down. Now the exercise you need to do is perform this analysis against the customer you service. And, the SWOT analysis must be displayed visually and not just words.

Business instant messaging

Once upon a time, instant messaging was restricted to chat rooms, and you needed special accesses and moderator's approval to enter into the world of chatting. Things are not restricted anymore. Chatting has become the most popular communication among general public and widely used in corporations. You can visualize chat as a telephone call, where the words spoken are in the written form instead of spoken. It can also be looked as an extension to e-mailing where the communication is no longer passive, and information exchange happens instantaneously.

There are pros and cons coming out of business instant messaging—instant messaging in companies. There are numerous good things. Productivity increases immeasurably when communication takes place through an instant messenger. While one can communicate while multi-tasking, the response to the information sought is almost immediate. There is no dedicated time that needs to be spent on communication like with telephones and you don't have to wait for the other party to respond unlike e-mails. It's a win-win from both angles. On the flipside, instant messaging could lead to conflicts. As messages tend to brief, and concentration divided with other activities, the sincerity and an attempt to answer the query does not come out the way it should.

Instant messaging is a key tool in organizations. It must be used the right way to gain maximum benefits, and if things tend to go haywire, consequences are potentially irreversible. In the following section, we explore some best practices to follow to obtain the best results out of this form of communication.

Business instant messaging etiquette

Here are some tips on instant messaging in businesses:

> ➤ If you are using a public instant messaging system like Skype, it is advisable to create a new ID that reflects your association with your organization and the screen name with a professional connotation.

> ➤ If you are walking away from your desk, be sure to set the status as *away*. It is annoying to see people as available and not respond. Likewise, if you are busy and do not want to be disturbed, select the appropriate status to set the right expectations.

> ➤ Begin an instant messaging conversation with a greeting such as *good morning* or *hi* followed by the first name. And, end the conversation by saying goodbye or thanking the other party.

> ➤ When you chat with a customer, be courteous and polite. Use phrases such as "how may I help you?", "thank you for sharing your feedback", and "let me consult my manager and get back to you by this evening".

> ➤ Do not use slang, for example "LOL" and "BRB". As a general rule, stay away from abbreviations that include EOD and FYI as well.

> ➤ Use complete words and sentences, rather than short forms such as come hr, gr8, and welcum bck.

> ➤ Instant messaging has a personal touch compared to telephones and e-mails, and for a professional cause, addressing each other in first and second person narration does the trick. For example, "I will check and let you know." or "Can you click on the icon on your desktop?"

> ➤ The font and color that is used must reflect corporate culture. I suggest Verdana or Book Antiqua, size 10, 11 or 12, in black.

> ➤ Using simple smileys are OK. But, the dancing ones and the ones that displays other emotions is a big no-no.

> ➤ Acknowledge every instant message with an *ok*, or something appropriate. Do not use responses such as ahhh, oh no, and hmmm.

> ➤ It is good etiquette to seek permission before you start chatting. Something like "Is it a good time to chat with you for a few minutes?" is absolutely fine.

> ➤ When a customer is chatting with you, stop communicating with others. Interchanging messages between windows and paying partial attention can land you in trouble.

Social media communication

Social media is the latest thing that most of us are hooked onto. The networks created on social media start out with personal contacts and then spread over to professional and extended friend circles. The catch is that everybody in the network is able to see what you post. And, many a time, employees in IT fail to distinguish between confidential information that has restricted control within company networks and this information can get propagated into personal and friends' circles, thereby causing a potential threat to the company.

Not only this, when social media is mixed between professional and personal contacts, professional contacts are able to see your personal antics, which can potentially reflect badly on the organization you work with.

What happens in the office stays in the office. Do not write about it elsewhere, especially on channels that are over the Internet. You must never share about what is happening in your office to the outside world. For example, "Delayed at work. Working on a proposal for Company A" read one of the updates from an employee of a competitor's organization. Our organization did not know that the client company was looking for certain services, which we incidentally offered too. We immediately contacted the client company to throw our hat in the race too. A naive mistake made by the employee cost the company an illustrious contract.

Keep professional and personal contacts on different networks preferably to avoid embarrassing situations for yourself and for your employer. Your customer need not know that you had too much to drink last night and imagine if there is an early morning meeting scheduled with them. Forget customers, if you have your boss on your network, your boss will know what you do when you take off, and this could perhaps reflect badly on the relationship between the two of you. The best way to deal with this, as I mentioned earlier, is to maintain separate networks and don't mix the two. It's like drinking. You must never mix different types of drinks in the same session.

Google Plus allows you to maintain various circles, which can be particularly useful in keeping distinct networks and posting specific updates to networks of your choice. Or, keep all your professional contacts on LinkedIn and personal ones on Facebook to avoid crisscrossing updates between various groups of contacts.

Action Point

Exercise (for readers to attempt at the end of this topic followed by a group discussion):

- List out all the social networks that you are a part of. Go through the list of contacts for each of your networks and identify personal and professional contacts. Segregate them and be aware of which updates are communicated to which groups on the network.

Summary

As this chapter ends, you are expected to know the following:

- All written communication come under one of the four forms:
    - Action-focused communication form to indicate actions to be performed
    - Influential communication to lead the recipient into your way of thinking
    - Negative communication to communicate unfavorable information
    - Information communication that plainly states facts
- Introduced the term jargons, and highlighted on situations when to employ them and when not to
- Style of providing project updates to customers and to peers
- Nuances of e-mail communication:
    - E-mail policy and introduction to a sample e-mail policy document
    - E-mail etiquette for effective use of e-mails
    - E-mail templates along with pointers for drafting templates
- Importance of visual communication and introduction to sequential flowcharts, hierarchical flowcharts, tables, and graphs
- Role of business instant messaging in IT
    - Business instant messaging etiquette for effective use of chat engines
- Effective use of social media communication

In the next chapter, we will specifically look at communicating over the telephone. We will discuss about the importance of listening before speaking and tips for improving listening skills. Also, the chapter covers scripts that can be used for standardizing communication over the telephone along with role play exercises. We will also discuss the power of questioning, which is key to getting the right and complete information before responding back.

> 4

Listening and Questioning for Effective Communication

Verbal communication is not all about talking fluently and intonation. There are precursors or catalysts that make verbal communication effective. In this chapter, we will deep dive into the art of listening and the power behind asking the right questions.

Unless you listen to the person you are speaking with, there is no way you would be able to understand what the requirements are, and when you start responding, you would either be preaching to the choir or generating little interest with the recipient.

As I have stated earlier, communication is an exchange of information. If the information coming from the other end does not satisfy your sensors, then you need to step up and bring the information out that is hidden deep in the crevices of the communicator. To do this, you need to ask questions.

The topics covered in this chapter are the ammunition you need to be effective communicators, and without which the shallowness of your communication stands exposed.

Listening – core of communication

Listening is the core of communication. If there is no listening involved, it is no longer communication. Instead, it merely becomes an act where the words you speak hit the walls and the flooring, and go into oblivion. If there is no listening involved, there is no recipient. In communication, you need to have both the communicator and recipient for it to happen.

When people speak, do you hear them or do you listen to them? When you hear people speak, you are basically acknowledging the words that are being said. Period. When you listen to people speak, you make sense of the things stated, the way it was delivered, and decipher the hidden meaning.

The truth is that we are taught in schools to read and write, but not to listen. Society judges us on the basis of what and how we speak, so we tend to do more speaking but not listening, which potentially fuels speaking.

It is a well-known fact that people who are good with relationships and rapport with other people are great listeners. It is their keen listening skills that have helped them garner the support. I discussed in *Chapter 1, Communication Training*, that relationships and rapport are a must for good communication, and here I further reiterate that to build it, you need to be a good listener, whether you like it or not.

To emphasize further on relationships playing a pivotal role in good communication, when you listen intently to what is being said, you earn the respect of the speaker. The speaker would be eager to reciprocate this gesture by listening to what you have to say when it is your turn. This game of giving and taking respect through listening is a great catalyst for improving communication and reducing conflict. Furthermore, only upon listening actively will you put yourself in a position to respond appropriately.

Hindrances to good listening

Let me ask you a few questions. When you are in a conversation, are you waiting for the speaker to stop so you can put out your thoughts that are hovering inside your head? Are you physically in a meeting and mentally elsewhere? Are you multitasking when you are talking over a telephone? Are you not interested in the content of the communication? I know the answers to these questions. It's *yes*. We have all been there, and the situations these questions present make us bad communicators and horrible listeners.

We are not inherently bad listeners. A number of factors, influences, situations, and people put us in a position of bad listening. I am not passing the buck to external factors but merely stating the facts so that we become aware of the distracting thoughts that can hinder us from being good communicators.

In the next few sections, I will state the common barriers to listening, and provide a way out, followed by an exercise.

Physical distractions

During a conversation, it is common for us to get distracted with the sounds that creep into the meeting rooms such as a bird tweeting or a janitor using the vacuum cleaner, smells emanating in the room, and fellow employees visible through the window, among other interesting factors.

If the distraction is one-fold, in a face-to-face meeting, the distractions get replicated multifold when you are having a conversation over the phone. It is accepted that it is difficult to keep physical distractions away when you are not being watched by the communicator.

The solution

These distractions are often felt by the speaker as well. The speaker can continue communicating, and you getting distracted is not a valid excuse. If there are sounds that are getting in the way of hearing what the communicator has to say, you can always ask them to wait until the noise is out of the way—like a jet flying at a low altitude.

For other distractions that are a result of you paying more attention to the windows and the birds singing, you are required to bring your senses under your control and pay complete attention to the communication in play. What you need is a commitment from yourself that you are going to listen in, no matter what the distracting forces are up to.

If your communication is via the telephone, the chances of distractions are much more, which means that you need to expend additional will power to concentrate on the words and the tone. Remember, if you are getting distracted by the noise that creeps into the telephone lines, interrupt the communicator and recommend that all the parties dialing in disconnect and reconnect. Communicators will rather be happy than annoyed to hear that people on the other line are keenly listening in and would like to get the best out of the time spent.

Action Point

Exercise (for students to attempt at the end of this topic followed by a group discussion):

- Share your individual / group experiences of getting distracted while on calls and in meetings. For every instance stated, discuss how it could have been overcome.

Mental distractions

While physical distractions have a trigger outside of ourselves, mental distractions are self-triggered and are dangerous to the extent that you would not realize that you are getting distracted, and are under the assumption that all is well.

Thinking of a new car that you booked last night, dwelling on the fight you had with your spouse this morning, cursing your ill luck on the missed promotion opportunity are some examples that can play on our minds while we go ahead with our day-to-day activities.

The solution

Let me tell you upfront that mental distractions are the most difficult to deal with. They sits on you like a parasite until you make a conscious effort to reduce their effect.

Before you get into meetings, make up your mind that the only thing you are going to concentrate on is what is being said in the meeting and nothing else. Convince yourself that this meeting is critical and you have no way out but to wear mental blinders and listen in.

Action Point

Exercise (for students to attempt at the end of this topic followed by a group discussion):

- Share your individual / group experiences of getting distracted while on calls and in meetings. For every instance stated, discuss how it could have been overcome.

Preconceived notions

During any communication session, if you believe that you already know the content that will be communicated, it is common to convince yourself that you know what will be said, and you have nothing to gain out of it, you will end up not listening. Why waste energy in listening to what I already know, you convince yourself. This generally happens when the speaker is well-known to the listener.

The solution

The problem here is that you are assuming that you know what will be said, which isn't necessarily true unless the speaker has conferred with you on the topics and content that will be discussed. Every conversation brings in a new learning for us, whether it is from a CEO of an organization or a subordinate.

If you are in a meeting, make sure you are very much in the meeting. Keep your egotistic instincts in a far place if you intend to be a lifelong learner, which I assume to be true since you are going through this workshop. Come with an open mind, listen without judging—once again with an open mind, and when the speaker is through, feel free to rifle through your notes to come up with your thoughts on the matter. Unless and until you have heard the whole nine yards, do not pre-conceive your thoughts. Remember that coming into a meeting with a closed mind is not the right framework for listening and learning.

Action Point

Exercise (for students to attempt at the end of this topic followed by a group discussion):

- Pick up a couple of technical or management topics that are well-known to all team members. Nominate one person as the speaker while the rest would be recipients. Ask the speaker to make an outline of what they are going to speak on, and let the rest of the team come up with their assumptions on what will be spoken. Compare the two sets of data and conclude that although the topic was common to both sets of parties, there were things stated that were outside the imagination of listeners and some assumed items were not included in the talk.

Opinions

You seem to have opinions when the speaker is in the middle of the conversation. You want to put across your thoughts at an (in)opportune moment. So, you wait until there is a pause and you start putting in your two cents—whether it is the right juncture or not, irrespective of whether the speaker is covering the same topic or not, you want to poke in your nose and blurt it out. In this process, you totally forget there is some information that is being conveyed, and you are not listening. You are filled with your opinions and your eye is only on the prize—the moment to speak your side of the story.

The solution

The root cause of this problem is not your opinion but that you don't respect the speaker. You don't believe that there is something of value that the speaker can deliver, and believe that your opinion matters a whole lot more than what the speaker has to say. Also, there is that ego factor that wants to outsmart the speaker. You opine to show everyone present, including the speaker, that you are the smart one (and not the person who is entrusted to speak).

Opinions are good. In fact, nobody should accept any information at face value. Information must be deciphered, analyzed, and if satisfied, fed to the memory banks for storage. But, there is a process for forming your opinion. The process states that you need to listen to everything that the speaker has to say and then form your opinions. You must not come up with your opinions or judge the speaker based on partial information. Only a fool would form opinions based on partial information. So, listen to everything that the speaker has to say, word by word, read between the lines, read the confidence levels in the gestures and doing all this will arm you better for forming the right opinions.

Action Point

Exercise (for students to attempt at the end of this topic followed by a group discussion):

- Imagine that you are in the midst of a speaking assignment. If you are being cut off before you finish speaking, how do you feel? Do you feel motivated and energized to continue speaking knowing fully well that listeners would rather interrupt before you finish sharing your ideas rather than listening to you?

- Listen to an audiobook or any other video training program on the topic that you are familiar with. Try not to judge the program until you have listened to it fully. Once you are done, write a small summary of what you have learned and your opinion of it. You are most likely to find that you have learned something new from it, even though you are familiar with the topic. Discuss your experience with the group after going through this activity.

Language and culture

Everything that the speaker says is zipping past your ears. Somehow you are not able to follow up with what is being said. Reasons could be plenty—usage of technical jargons, accent, speed, and volume, among others.

The solution

When I was in college, I had a professor who was from Chinese descent. I had a hard time following him the first few classes as he spoke with a thick accent and spoke too fast for my liking. I noticed that some of the other multicultural students were sitting in the front rows and nodding their heads while I was in one of the rear benches. So, I decided to move to the front and the experience was something else. I understood the speaker better than before.

The way I found a workaround, was that you must make an effort to follow the speaker. Accent and speed of delivery is innate and more often than not cannot be changed overnight. It takes practice to understand certain accents. In my professional career, when I first started working with UK clients, I had a hard time following their English. I had worked with American clients all my life, lived in the US for a few years and watched Hollywood movies. Americanized English was my familiar ground. I stuck the telephone literally into my ear, blurred the distractions around me, closed my eyes, and concentrated on everything that was said. Within a few weeks, I was able to follow their English with eyes open and on speakerphone. There are no shortcuts; you just need to do the initial frequency sync with people of different accents.

If the speaker is using too much technical jargon, you can always ask it to be broken down in a simpler way. If you are a designated listener, there is nothing wrong is asking to be explained in a different way. It is your right. The same concept goes with the volume of the speakers. Many speakers don't check with the listeners whether they are being heard, which, for a speaker, is not a good etiquette.

Multitasking

You are known as a superstar in your office. Somebody who completes designated work ahead of schedule. What is your secret? You multitask. You perform two to three activities at any given time. If I was to ask you whether you were effective, your manager can give a thumbs-up. But, when I probe further about the understanding you obtained from the meetings that you attended, the effectiveness drops just as Lucifer fell from God's grace. Your presence is recorded but the content of the discussion did not sink in. When your manager asks you to explain, you say that you were preparing the weekly reports while you were on the meeting call. You were present on the call but not *listening*.

The solution

The problem that is reported in this hindrance is very common in the IT industry. Many attend meetings because they are on the invite list, or their manager has asked them to be on the bridge call. You respond when your name is called out, and more often than not, you ask the question posed at you to be repeated.

There are many reasons why you are not listening in:

> ➤ You are not interested in the discussion. You are here only because of your manager and it is your job to answer the questions when asked.

> ➤ You are a multitasker, especially when it is a telephone meeting. You are doing something else while other parties are talking.

> ➤ The content of the meeting is too simple or too hard for you to follow.

> ➤ You choose to listen selectively. When certain keywords pop up, your senses come back to life.

If you are not an active participant, let the chairperson know. So, when they need you in the meeting, they can call out your name or ask you to dial in when needed. Staying on the call the whole time is a waste of resources that offices can potentially save.

If you are in a meeting as an active participant, do not multitask. It is unhealthy to be present in meetings while your mind (and body) is elsewhere. Decide what type of participant you are, and take an appropriate course of action.

Tips for improving your listening skills

Remember that improving your listening skills will improve your overall communication. One does not go without the other. Here is a list of tips that you can start practicing to improve your listening skills.

> ➤ Pay complete attention to the speaker and the words spoken and unspoken. Try not to get distracted by the forces of nature or man-made distractions.

> ➤ Maintain eye contact with the speaker the whole time. This will alleviate the distractions and will help you concentrate. Secondly, the speaker will feel at ease that you are indeed listening in.

> ➤ Don't let your mind wander to far off places while you are present in a meeting. It is natural for us to think of our own car ride when the speaker shares his own experience. Stay focused and glued to what the speaker has to say.

> ➤ Acknowledge when the speaker looks at you by nodding. If you are on a call, a simple OK in between will not keep the speaker second-guessing whether they are being heard or not.

> ➤ Take notes. Note taking is a good way of following up with the speaker. It is believed that most of the things we hear are washed away unless there is an emotional attachment to it. So, take notes, so you recharge your memory cells through your notes.

> ➤ Keep an open mind and do not form opinions in the midst of the session. Extract everything you can, as long as the speaker is talking. Once done, you must go through your notes and come up with your questions, objections, and opinions.

> ➤ Do not judge the speaker, or do not carry prejudice to the meetings. These will hinder you from listening to the words, tones, and the unsaid.

> ➤ Ask questions if you are not clear on things stated. Do not assume that you will self-research on the topic at a later time.

> ➤ If the speaker is using jargon or is speaking too fast, request that the content be simplified and the pace be lowered for better understanding. No speaker will take offense to this.

> ➤ Stay relaxed. For communication to be effective, you need to relax and keep emotions such as anger out to create an environment for effective communication—which starts with listening.

Action Point

Exercise (for students to attempt at the end of this topic followed by a group discussion):

> ■ Next time you are in a meeting or in training, follow the listening etiquettes, and share your experience with the rest of the group on how different it felt compared to the earlier ways.

Power of questioning

Listening is the medium of receiving information. Not all received information is perfect and usable. Often, the message needs further uncovering, to be looked at from various perspectives, and to be deciphered. This set of information can be obtained, more often than not, by the power of questioning.

During and after the process of listening, for communication to be effective, you need to pepper it with relevant questions; questions that are not aimed at proving your smartness, but rather with the sole intent of getting useful information that can be used constructively.

Benefits of asking questions

In a number of ways, the type of questions that can be asked will vary. Asking questions is a subjective matter. It will be decided on a case-to-case basis. I cannot possibly point out what questions to ask but rather orient you towards asking relevant questions and highlighting the benefits that can be directly derived out of asking good quality questions.

> ➤ Getting confirmation of what the speaker is saying. You can rephrase in your own way and check if you understood the matter rightly.

➤ You can obtain more information than originally offered by asking open-ended questions—why is it beneficial for us to study yoga?

➤ By asking questions, good discussions usually emerge. The speaker and other group members might indulge in brain picking, which will further help in obtaining various perspectives.

➤ Managers can ask leading questions to subordinates to obtain the favored response, and simultaneously make it look like a group decision. Two birds with a single arrow—don't you think we should opt for supplier A over the rest in the race?

➤ One way you can build rapport is by asking the right questions, questions that can tell the speaker that you are curious about learning more.

➤ Probe further in getting to a piece of information that the communicator is not voluntarily ready to divulge—can you tell me why the poles of the sun switch every eleven years?

➤ At times, you can alleviate destructive emotions by asking questions such as "what kind of service would have pleased you?"

Action Point

Exercise (for students to attempt at the end of this topic followed by a group discussion):

■ Share your experience when you have asked the right question and have obtained the answers you were seeking.

There are some ill effects of questioning if the process is misused. Smart Alecs like to ask questions that they have an answer to only to demonstrate their knowledge if the speaker fails to answer. This is quite common in the IT world, where the constant rat race prompts people to outdo one another. Furthermore, questions can also be used to mock the communicator—don't you know the abbreviation of this term? You are not becoming an effective communicator using questions in a derogatory manner, but rather breaking the relationship. Through questions, do not degrade anybody. Use it as a powerful tool that can give you tangible benefits rather than brownie points.

Various questioning techniques

Not all questions are the same. In some questions, you warrant a single word answer, and in some, you pick the brain of the speaker. So, the questioning technique is about asking the right type of question in a given scenario. *You don't want to arm yourself with a knife in a gun fight!*

Probing technique

In the probing technique, the speaker is not eager to give out information. You need to ask the right question, support your questions with logic, and put the speaker on the spot to give you the answer that you require. Detectives commonly use this technique on suspects, victims, and witnesses.

In this technique, the skill is to start asking non-pointed question, and based on the answer you receive ask pointy questions, which helps you delve further.

There is a probing technique in IT called the *5 why* analysis which is popularly used by teams that work on risk and security management areas. The technique is a series of why questions that you pose to dig deeper into the dirt. The idea is that by the time you are done with the fifth why, you would have obtained the root cause, which is the desired information. Here's a small illustration.

A computer is infected with a virus. The technical team that is responsible for managing computers is not providing a whole lot of information on this issue. You are an IT information security officer and it is your job to find the root cause for this issue. You begin asking the questions this way:

1st Why: Why was the computer infected with a virus?

Answer: The user was not using an anti-virus protection application

2nd Why: Why was the user not using an anti-virus protection application?

Answer: It was not installed on the computer

3rd Why: Why was it not installed on the computer?

Answer: Due to human error

In this example, we got the answer we were looking for in the third why. In reality, you can go with as many whys as possible.

Action Point

Exercise (for students to attempt at the end of this topic followed by a group discussion):

- Pick up any breakdown that you have faced in your organization. Apply the 5-why technique to get down to the root of the issue.
- Do you think asking probing questions to those who are close to you would strain the relationship that you enjoy? Reason out. There are pros and cons with probing questions. The downside is that the person who you are posing it to might take offense due to lack of trust. So, the idea is to use it wisely.

Open-ended questions

If the intention of asking questions is to engage the recipient into opening up by sharing thoughts and perspectives, you must ask open-ended questions. The answers to open ended questions can never be a single word. What is your opinion on the world's economy? For this question, the answer will be as detailed as possible, thereby giving way for conversation to continue. Suppose if the same question was to be phrased something like—Do you think the world's economy is sinking? The answer could be yes or a no and that can also play spoilsport in killing the conversation.

You need to engage open-ended questions when you need details. They are designed to extract information. As a classic example, on romantic dates, couples generally ask open-ended questions. Share your experience on the rafting trip you undertook last year. What are your color preferences? If they were to start asking each other closed questions, they will end up playing the game of *twenty questions*.

Closed questions

Closed questions have its place in communication. The conversation killer is not a villain in the world of communication. Closed questions are employed when confirmation is needed, where a yes or a no would suffice. In IT organizations, customer satisfaction is generally built on closed ended questions. Did you enjoy the level of service you obtained today?

Closed questions play a major part in surveys and business analytics. These mediums employ closed questions in getting standardized answers from respondents—Do you prefer a smartphone or a smart watch? Options: a. Smartphone b. Smart watch c. Both in combination d. Don't know. Based on the standardized answer from the available options, business analysts can derive valuable business intelligence that aids improvements in the IT industry.

Action Point

Exercise (for students to attempt at the end of this topic followed by a group discussion):

- Provide a few more circumstances when you would ask open ended and closed questions.

Leading questions

If the speaker intends to build consensus on a point and get everybody to agree on their thinking, they should ask leading questions in a way that doesn't make it look obvious (and devious). Many successful managers and leaders have used this technique successfully to get what they want, and have made it look like their subordinates and followers came up with the decision. When teams agree on an approach to follow, rather than being dictated by a manager, the decision taken by the team is sufficient to motivate them in the right direction. The manager need not put in any extra efforts in motivating their team into getting things done.

When you ask leading questions, make sure that they are closed questions. The listeners must not have multiple choices to choose from. If you give an open platform to them, they will rule the roost. When you are dealing with customers, if you want them to buy into your ideas, provide them with the benefits of your product, and lead them into asking—Don't you think this product is perfect for your organization?

Action Point

Exercise (for students to attempt at the end of this topic followed by a group discussion):

- It is widely believed that leading questions is an act of deception and judicial courts across the world disallow lawyers from asking leading questions. What are your thoughts?

Summary

As this chapter ends, you should know more about the following:

- ➤ Importance of listening
- ➤ Awareness of various hindrances to listening effectiveness
- ➤ Tips to improve listening skills
- ➤ Importance and benefits of asking the right questions
- ➤ Questioning techniques

In the next chapter, we will specifically look at communicating over the telephone. The chapter covers scripts that can be used for standardizing communication over the telephone along with role play exercises. We will also discuss the power of questioning which is key to getting the right and complete information before responding back.

> 5
Telephone Communication

Verbal communication is complicated in its own right. It has a number of spokes that make it seem effective—the words spoken, voice intonation, body language, and facial expressions to state a few. Going by the quality definition as stated in *Chapter 1, Communication Training*, face-to-face communication where the communicator and recipients sit across physically from one another is the best form of verbal communication as the communicator gets an opportunity to communicate using all the aspects of verbal communication—spoken words, tone, body language, and facial expressions. But is it practical these days? With widening workforces and serving customers across continents, does it make logical sense for people to be physically present in a room for every meeting?

There needs to be a compromise made to make pragmatic sense of communication. The compromise comes in the form of telephones, where the communicator has only the spoken words and the voice tone to play with, but instead, is saving a bunch of time which would have involved the logistics of getting in and out of a discussion room.

In this chapter, I will primarily discuss telephone communication. I will focus on the specific elements that are crucial for effective communication on the phone, such as the use of language and tone of voice.

Telephonic communication

Today, a voice call need not be on a telephone alone. Most organizations employ **Voice over IP technology (VoIP)**, which enables us to place and receive calls through our computers. The introduction of VoIP technology has made voice communication informal, in comparison to how it was viewed at one time. Earlier, when calls came through a telephone, we used to start with a greeting—at least by introducing ourselves. Thanks to VoIP, the professional greeting is replaced by an informal one—*what's up?* I am not saying this is wrong, but the changing trend is affecting the way we handle our professional calls that land on our telephone lines as well.

In an IT organization, there are mainly two channels of telephonic communication:

> ➤ Communication between employees of an organization
> ➤ Communication between employees and customers

Before I get into the channel specifics, there are a few common denominators that I want to address first.

#1: When you make a call, be prepared

I am certain all of us have taken calls where the party on the other end knows what needs to be said but has not figured out yet how to say it. I am not talking about the people who beat around the bush before bringing up the topic that's the reason behind the call. I am referring to people who start out uncertainly, go in a certain direction, retract, give a few pauses, and then take another track. In the end, the unprepared caller has wasted both your time and their time, and has left a bad taste in the mouth of the person at the receiving end. Imagine if this happens to a customer.

The point being, if you are the caller, come prepared. Before you make the call, know what you are going to talk about, how you are going to say it, and the path you are going to undertake in jumping from one topic to another.

I for one like to write down what I am going to talk about in my notebook, and I also write down the sequence of topics that I would like to bring to the table. This gives me the confidence of being in charge of the call. For example, let's say I want to call my customer with the following agenda:

1. Explore new business
2. Understand the pulse of the customer
3. Seek approval for a downtime of services

The call will progress along the following lines:

Abhinav: Hi, Mike. This is Abhinav from ABC Technologies. Is this a good time to talk for a few minutes?

Mike (customer): Sure. No problem.

Abhinav: I am sorry that I called without prior notice. A pressing situation has come up and I needed to discuss it with you.

Mike: That's okay. I can talk now.

Abhinav: One of the servers in the data center needs patching. A security patch has been released and we don't want to delay deploying it. So, we were planning on doing it over the weekend. Emails would be affected at the most for an hour, but we hope to complete it well within the hour. Are you okay with this?

Mike: I think one hour outage should be fine. Email me the specifics and I will relay it to others here.

Abhinav: Wonderful. I will send you an email with all the details. And, it has been some time since we spoke. How are you finding our services? All OK?

Mike: Yes yes. Everything is fine except for the delay in project A. But I guess that didn't impact us too much though.

Abhinav: Yes. I am aware of the delay, and we have already taken preventive steps to ensure that similar delays are avoided.

Mike: Good!

Abhinav: I also heard about your new acquisition. The acquisition gives you a better hold over the region doesn't it?

Mike: Yes. You are right. It does. It was a good strategic move for us. And, it all worked out well.

Abhinav: Wonderful. You need us to help you out with the additional resources you are getting from it?

Mike: Yes. We were discussing integrating the environments. So, let's discuss the specifics next week.

Abhinav: Sounds like a plan. I will check with your assistant and book a slot next week.

Mike: Good. I will let her know my preferences.

Abhinav: Thanks Mike. We will talk next week. Have a great weekend.

Mike: You too. Bye.

This transcript is in fact from one of my meetings earlier this year. I had listed down the topics to bring up in a specific order and it came out just the way I intended. My notes looked something like this:

Downtime needed. Security patch. Important. One hour.

Pulse check. Project A delay—procurement process overshot the plan. New process in place.

New acquisition. Strong player in the market. Expansion of services.

A word of caution. At times, you may have prepared with notes such as I did, but the discussion may not go as intended. It may take a turn where the customer might start asking for specifics for which you are not prepared for. In such cases, you need to improvise. One way of doing this is by expanding on your notes by planning in detail—if the customer says this, then I will say this, else I will say something else. You get the idea?

#2: Professional yet friendly

No, professionalism and friendliness are not two sides of a coin. Both can co-exist at the same time, and the combination if applied well is deadly in a good way. In a telephonic conversation, the person on the other side of the phone can hear your voice only and nothing else. So, whatever you want to express, you need to do it with your voice—whether you smile, frown, or respect.

When you speak on a call, be warm and friendly and speak wholeheartedly to the person. Yet, at the same time, stay within the boundaries of work and focused. You can display friendliness by staying enthusiastic about the conversation and showing genuine interest in what is being said. If you are disinterested, don't put up a face, but rather find a way to curtail it without being obtrusive about it.

When I say professional, I am only talking about the limits that we need to impose. The limits are generally work related, without bringing up personal tastes, topics, and derogatory statements.

When I worked with some customers from Australia, they appended the word *mate* during conversations, and this brought about a sense of friendliness. The discussions revolved around projects and services, and at times, the weather, food, and weekend plans. We never ventured into talking behind people's backs or discussing topics in a derogatory sense. The discussions were always above the table and professional. By the end of the month, I knew that my customer had two daughters and a wife who loved Indian food.

Through my experience, I want to highlight how friendliness and professionalism can co-exist, and I'm not indicating that you are expected to know the customer as a friend. No, you are not expected to be your customer's friend, but the warmth in your voice must comfort the person to open up, and tell you everything without withholding any information due to lack of trust.

#3: Stay positive

Don't be misguided by the topic heading and think that I have started teaching psychology 101. Staying positive means being approachable and not finding the fastest way to end a conversation.

Consider the following hypothetical transcript:

> *Abhinav: Hi, Mike. This is Abhinav from ABC Technologies. I called to tell you that the server has been successfully patched.*
>
> *Mike: Good. I had something else to ask you. The delay on project A delivery. Can you tell me where the delay was ebbing from?*
>
> *Abhinav: Aaah…. I don't know.*
>
> *Mike: OK?*
>
> *Silence*
>
> *Mike: I want to know the reasons for delay. Send me a report detailing the cause for the delay. I would like to have it within the next hour. Thanks!*

What is wrong with it? Everything. I didn't know the causes for the project's delay, which is reasonable. But, I further pulled myself down by saying that I don't know what the reasons are. This told the customer that I was evading the topic by playing ignorance. What was the end result? The customer was upset, and I had a stringent deadline for giving him the data that he needed. Perhaps the customer may never see me as before, and will look down upon me every time I speak to him. Not good.

If I could go back in a time machine and redo the conversation, this is how it would have gone:

> *Abhinav: Hi Mike. This is Abhinav from ABC Technologies. I called to tell you that the server has been successfully patched.*
>
> *Mike: Good. I had something else to ask you. The delay on project A delivery. Can you tell me where the delay was ebbing from?*
>
> *Abhinav: Mike, let me get the details and email them to you today.*
>
> *Mike: No problem. I have to present a report to the board on the outage. As you know, the delay cost us some business and this got the board interested in the matter.*
>
> *Abhinav: I understand that the delay has impacted you financially. I will send the report at the earliest.*
>
> *Mike: Sure. You can send it to me by the end of this week. I am not expected to report it until Wednesday next week.*
>
> *Abhinav: Thanks Mike. Have a good day!*

How different was this? And, the only difference in the conversation is my attitude. Although I did not know the cause of delay, I proactively volunteered to obtain the details. And, the customer opened up and told me why he needed it, and the timeframes as well were not too stringent.

To reiterate, never say *I don't know* to the customer. But, that should not stop you from saying *no*. Some believe that if we say *no*, then it counts as negativity, so they avoid saying *no* and fall into bottomless pits. Say it when necessary—like when a customer demands services that are outside the contract. Saying no and *I don't know* are two different things. The first has to be embraced with prudence and the second avoided.

Employee-employee telephonic communication

There was a time when I interacted more with my colleagues sitting in a different office than my family who stayed under the same roof. This is certainly the case with most IT professionals. The job demands constant communication and coordination with other colleagues, and perhaps this is the sole reason why many organizations subscribe to team building activities.

With colleagues, the three common denominators that I discussed at the beginning of this topic apply just as well. Although I mostly mentioned about customers, you can just as well substitute customers with colleagues and the principles will not change. Fellow employees enjoy working at a friendly cum professional level, so well prepared telephonic communications that are treated appreciably and positivity increase the mutual trust and respect between individuals.

In this section, I will highlight certain types of interactions that are common in the IT industry and provide a few specific tips on how telephonic communication must happen. There are numerous other exchanges that you can apply based on the principles that I am about to share in this section.

Work handover

In IT, handing over work from one employee to another is common. Work changes hands constantly, at various stages of a project or a service. Data flow between entities (design to deployment), performance (from functional manager to people manager), and work handover between shifts are just a few examples.

At the core, work handover revolves around exchanging information from one entity to another. As IT is all about information, there is prime importance given to information exchanges such as this. If the exchange is inaccurate, it is possible that projects may not succeed and customer satisfaction may take a hit. So, to state plainly, work handovers are critical.

There are a number of ways to do this. Any medium can be used to hand over work. But, for effective handovers, follow the method that I recommend based on my ground-level experience.

The data that needs to be handed over must be written down in a document or an email. Writing helps in reflecting on thoughts and putting down information that has been given some thought. After putting it in words, share the document with the person receiving the handover. And then call this person to go through the document that you have prepared. While you explain the document, the person receiving it has the benefit of listening to you and reading through it as well. This two-dimensional approach helps in effectively communicating work handover information. But wait, there's more. While the person handing over explains the written content, the data goes through another round of validation and perhaps the person receiving it can probe further to get information that may have been left out.

Action Point

Exercise (for students to attempt at the end of this topic followed by a group discussion):

- How is work handed over from one team to another, or one employee to another, in your organization? If there are no face-to-face or telephonic handovers, how effective is it?

Support request

Not everybody in IT is omniscient. In fact, I can be certain to state that none can boast knowing it all. At some point or another, we need to consult with others—request support.

The ideal way to consult with others is through a telephone. I am aware that some employees request support from others through an email or business instant messaging. But, these two non-verbal mediums are not always instantaneous, and it is the human tendency to ask for help at the last moment. If employees are collocated, then face-to-face trumps it all, including telephonic help being sought. But, we don't have this luxury anymore. Most of our teams sit elsewhere, and the best we can afford is a telephone, and we should go for the best option.

When you need help, you need it right away. First and foremost, when you speak to a person seeking help, the probability of denying support is minimal. And, the person asking for help can always confirm if the understanding is right. The feedback confirmation is critical in getting help, and the best way to get it if teams are not sitting together is through a telephone.

Action Point

Exercise (for students to attempt at the end of this topic followed by a group discussion):

- Let's say a colleague calls you and asks for your help in solving a problem that the colleague is facing. To show the solution, you must use a drawing tool to explain certain technicalities, but this is impossible over the telephone. What kind of a solution would you employ to alleviate this problem that telephonic communication comes with?

Telephonic meetings

Meetings are part and parcel of our IT lives. We meet to discuss, exchange views, and to improvise on work products. So, it is imperative that meetings are successful, especially the telephonic ones, and by now you know the reasons why I am stressing on telephonic meetings. The comfort of taking a phone call at our own desk is incomparable.

I have dedicated an entire section in the next chapter on meetings. Yet, I wanted to bring this topic here and discuss the specifics related to telephony.

If you are using a presentation in your meeting, the people sitting across and beside you can follow the slides on the screen and you can run through them in any fashion that you wish. But, when you have people who are blinded by distance and aided by telephonic technology, you need to put extra effort in reading out the slide numbers every time you jump to a new one.

When people sit across from you, you can read their body language and ask relevant follow up questions like "It seems something is unclear on this slide. Which part do you want me to repeat?" But the people on the other side are at a disadvantage. So, to minimize it, you need to ask after every slide whether they have questions that need to be addressed. Not all listeners speak up unless called out for. And, at the end of the day, meetings are conducted for everybody's benefit as effective information exchange leads to better work products and delivery.

Action Point

Exercise (for students to attempt at the end of this topic followed by a group discussion):

- What type of meetings do you prefer? Telephonic or face-to-face communication? Depending on the choice of your answer, what are the reasons for opting for one channel over the other and why is there a comfort level? (When I have asked this question to some of my teams, a few have stated telephonic and the comfort level is aided by online games that they can play during the call.)

Employee-customer telephonic communication

There is always something sacred about communication with customers. Every communication you make, you are either building the confidence levels of the customer or breaking them down. It cruelly seems like customer perception depends on communication rather than the actual work that is being carried out.

In any customer-IT organization relationship, there is a fair amount of transactions that happen over the telephone. Although the critical meetings are always held face to face, a number of ad-hoc and routine meetings are preferred to be run over the phone. And, these telephonic meetings often act as a precursor or post-meeting follow ups for the face-to-face critical meetings.

In this section, I am going to touch on understanding the customer's requirements, speaking in a language understood by the customer, and meeting the requirements.

Understand the customer's needs

To understand what the customer really needs, you need to (carefully) listen to what the customer has to say. Remember that the customer will not tell you the requirements in your language–with jargon. The customer states it the way it's seen by them, and there is a big difference when it comes to how they see it and how you vision it. So, you need to momentarily put yourself in their shoes and understand what they are trying to convey.

For example, a customer may call you and tell you that they are not able to receive emails on their system. So, you will start to think of all the things that make up the email solution and what could have gone wrong, either centrally or on the customer's system. But, what the customer could have probably missed telling you is that the email program is not running yet. This is a true incident experienced by one of my engineers.

In essence, you need to gauge the customer and the level of technicality they can go into and then start conversing at their level. If you find a tech savvy customer, then zip to the short forms that you generally use on the job.

Also, it is unlikely that you will understand the exact requirement in the first instance. You may need to probe further and ask the right questions. The topic of questioning comes into play in this case.

In the email incident that I mentioned earlier, if the engineer taking the phone call had (really) heard what the customer was saying, he would have perhaps deciphered that the email program wasn't open yet. The engineer could have further probed to check whether all the basic things were in place before moving into the specifics.

In short, when a customer states the requirement or a problem, you need to listen word for word and not use imagination and assumption to fill the void that customers create when they speak. Instead, fill the void by asking questions. Will you require support during off business hours? Are you trying to access the Internet within the office premises? Do you see the email program running and trying to fetch mails?

After listening and probing, still don't assume you know everything that the customer needs. Relay your understanding and let the customer confirm your understanding.

Conclude your understanding of the customer's requirements with empathy. If the caller is distraught that all the mails in the mailbox are lost, reassure that you will do your best to recover the lost mail. I am not stating that you make false promises, but rather be human and act human, the way you would if a friend was to share a problem with you. Do not act like a robot in getting the requirements and confirming them.

Action Point

Exercise (for students to attempt at the end of this topic followed by a group discussion):

- You are a customer who has called in to obtain certain information. You are told by the call center employee that the team that is responsible for answering this query has left for the day. You are not happy with it. Enact a role play, where one is a call center employee and the other is a customer. The objective behind this is to learn the importance of being flexible depending on how the call is progressing. The role play can be further expanded with various flavors such as the customer's query getting answered and the employee taking a long time to find the required information.

No jargon please

I have covered this topic in detail in an earlier chapter, but I want to reiterate it once more due to the gravity the topic carries. When you are speaking to a customer on the telephone, it is natural for us to envision the technical architectures, project deliverables, and IT problems in our own language, which is studded with technicalities, and relay the same set of words to the customer. It happens to all of us. So, we need to take extra precaution, especially over the telephone, since we do not have the time to think through our answers like in an email before replacing jargon with layman terms.

Action Point

Exercise (for students to attempt at the end of this topic followed by a group discussion):

■   Role play. Pick up a technical topic in your domain. Identify an employee in your organization who isn't technical, like those who are managers. The exercise is to call the manager and explain a technical solution, but in a language that the manager understands. After the call is complete, ask the manager to let you know what they understood. If what has been understood and what you said are a close match, you have successfully communicated jargon-filled expertise in plain English. And, you have a good future in dealing with customers and managing accounts.

Meeting the requirements

Once you understand your customer's requirements, you will have to follow the process of answering your customer's queries or fixing issues that may have cropped up. Well, this process will take its course, but what we are going to concentrate on is the communication aspect.

Set the expectations of the customer. If you are going to answer the query right away or fix their problems while they are connected on the call, that's all well and good. But, if you are going to need a couple of hours or a few days to respond to their queries or issues, tell them as such. Make sure you set the expectations correctly, and in the competition of making the customer excited, do not make false promises.

Suppose you set an expectation as the next business day, and even after diligently working towards the solution, you were not able to provide what the customer wanted. You will need to call the customer before your deadline ends and provide them the reasons why you were unable to resolve the problem, and then provide a new expectation.

Customers appreciate being informed about possible delays proactively rather than after the deadline has passed. Since all the communication happens over the telephone, it should not hinder you from making the calls as soon as you find out about a possible delay.

Telephony etiquette for effective communication

Here are some universally accepted telephone manners that are expected from each and every person in the professional world. This list is not comprehensive, but nevertheless, it covers most areas of telephonic communication:

> ➤ During the call, do not multitask. Even if you are working on something when the call comes in, stop everything and concentrate on the voice on the telephone.

> ➤ Do not read, chat on instant messengers, or eat while you are engaged in a telephonic conversation. In IT organizations, I have witnessed many professionals do these three activities the most while they are *supposedly* speaking to someone on their telephones.

> ➤ The tone of your voice must be pleasant and friendly. Even if you are bored to death or tired to slumber, cheer yourself up and be the friendliest voice one can hear on the other side.

> ➤ Your body language has a say in how your voice tone comes out. When you are taking a call, sit upright and the confidence is showcased through your voice.

> ➤ Clarity of speech is paramount. Remember that the person on the other end has only your voice as a means of communication. So, you need to speak slow and pronounce every word clearly.

> ➤ When you are making an outbound call, think about what you need to achieve out of it, what questions to ask, what information to obtain, and how to go about doing it.

> ➤ As you are aware, speaking on a telephone is a pleasurable task. So, don't beat around the bush, but instead come to the topic directly and be sure not to digress during the length of it.

> ➤ Most of us work on global projects, where customers sit in one part of the world, delivery takes place in another part, and some other teams are spread out across continents. When you are calling someone, be sure that you are not calling at odd hours. Keep a time-zone tool on your computer to aid you with this.

> ➤ It is good manners not to hang up before the customer does. So, even after you exchange your closure greetings with the customer, wait until the customer hangs up and then you follow suit.

Summary

As this chapter ends, you are expected to understand the following:

➤ Key principles of telephonic communication

➤ Telephonic communication between employees

➤ Telephonic communication between customers and employees

➤ Telephone etiquette

In the next chapter, we will discuss the nuances of face-to-face communication. It hovers around the various channels that exist in face-to-face communication, voice intonations, and facial expressions. We will take a deeper look into body language. Conflict management, a clean desk, and personal appearance are also discussed in this chapter.

> 6

Face-to-face Communication

Face-to-face communication is the earliest form of communication, and it is still the most preferred method. No matter how farther technology advances, we always have a special emotional appeal to this physical form of communication. Moreover, communicating directly has a personal touch and hence it is considered as the purest form of communication.

Perhaps the biggest advantage that face-to-face interaction has is the multiangular, multichannel communication aided through words, tone of voice, and the body language. Let's say you are talking to someone in person. He is sharing about the tragedies of his life. The tone of his voice and his body language must sync with the words stated. Based on all the factors, you will be in a good position to judge the integrity of the facts and the truth the message contains.

For the same reason, face-to-face communication is most effective compared over written or telephonic means. It utilizes all possible ammunition to pass the information. This can be demonstrated through sales activities. Most sales are done through face-to-face interactions. The best way to sell to a customer is by sitting across from them, and convincing them of the benefits of the product on hand. Even if the initial sales communication happens over a telephone or through an e-mail, closures are done physically. This goes on to show the effectiveness of this form of communication and the power behind the ancient method.

Yet we cannot employ the most effective form of communication owing to logistical and cost-effective measures. Companies must strike a balance and insist on physical interaction for priority meetings.

When to employ face-to-face communication

Although face-to-face communication is most effective and widely preferred, it cannot be practiced at every communication opportunity. It comes at a price, and the price is quite high—the cost of holding face-to-face meetings and the time on hand for all participants. Individuals must carefully prioritize their meetings, the important communication opportunities to leverage on face-to-face communication. Some examples are sales pitches, customer service reviews, and interviews. Yes, I did mention interviews knowing full well that most interviews are telephonic these days, and this is not good for the state of company affairs, hiring somebody who the company bosses have never met. I will keep this discussion for another day, for another book possibly.

Here is one of the methods of picking the interactions that are done face to face. Put down all the meetings you have on a calendar, and categorize them as routine, priority, and discretional:

> ➤ **Routine meetings** are mostly daily, weekly, and monthly scheduled meetings that you need to attend, because your company governance mandates you to attend. Your attendance is more important than your presence per se. These are the meetings that you can look to take up telephonically.

> ➤ Then you have **priority meetings** that mean the world to you. The outcome of the meeting has a bearing to you, your team, and to the organization. These are the meetings that have to be done in physical proximity. In priority interactions, you are required to bring your a-game onto the table, and make it count.

> ➤ Lastly you have **discretional meetings** where the word discretion does not refer to your participation in the meeting but rather to decide whether such meetings can be held over a telephone, chat, or face to face.

I earlier frowned upon conducting telephonic interviews. Yet, I would insist on initial telephonic interviews if there are multiple rounds to be held. I would opt for telephonic interviews to screen candidates for basic technical skills, but the rounds that involve testing analytical reasoning and the manager round (also referred to as the HR round in some organizations) where the attitude of the person is put to test are mandatorily in person.

I once interviewed a candidate over a telephone. Every time I asked a question, the candidate took some time to understand the question by repeating whatever I said and I could hear faint keyboard strokes. Then answers flowed like a river. I wasn't sure if he was *searching for answers to* my questions so I threw him a googly by asking a question based on a scenario and he came up blank. That confirmed my suspicions and therefore is a strong driver for opposing telephonic interviews.

Other benefits of face-to-face communication

I discussed the effectiveness and the personal touch that face-to-face communication brings to the table. There is more to it than meets the eye.

Humans are emotional creatures. If wavelengths match, we tend to be the best of friends, or conflicts arise out of every word uttered, eye contact, tone of voice, and other nonverbal aspects. Conflicts tend to grow on us, as the distance between the other person/people widens. The preferred method to resolve conflicts between the warring factions is to bring them across the table and put out everything that is there hidden in the subconscious. We employ these tactics whenever our subordinates have problems with other employees and vendors. We simply bring them to a meeting room and ask them to open up and then work over the differences. The results are simply amazing, as a number of conflicts are resolved and the effectiveness of our teams is better than ever before. We have tried the same formula over a telephone and it is all smoke and no fire.

When major decisions are to be taken in organizations, these meetings are mostly held in a face-to-face fashion. Yes, any conflicts coming out of the decision-making process can be quelled, but there is a higher stake in reaching consensus, and this is best achieved through physical proximity between leaders in the organization. In most cases, leaders head off to an offsite center, where they are farther away from office distractions, and interact at close proximity to come out with critical decisions that will be crucial for the company's future. It further connects the involved individuals and bonds them together for the betterment of the company they serve. Likewise, the employees that are undergoing this training can come together for a face-to-face brainstorming session to come out with team goals, discuss unrelenting issues, and sort out conflicts.

It is a fact in the IT world that collocated teams perform better compared to those spread across locations. The reason is the same as I stated earlier—personal relationships, bonds, and friendships are built when fellow employees see each other on a day-to-day basis. In an IT environment where work happens in the virtual world, let true dialog ride on face-to-face communication. It is OK to schedule meetings on e-mails and get a quick query sorted out over chat or telephone, but when an honest and truthful conversation like an appraisal meeting is needed, there is no substitute to sitting across from each other and talking it out. I have seen people who take the easy way out through e-mails, where they have all the time in the world to draft and redraft a dozen times. The outcome of this communication may not be from the heart but will certainly be affiliated to the e-mail and company etiquette. If true and honest dialog is what you seek, get the person to sit across the table from you and what follows is the antidote for the issues plaguing the team and the company.

Action Point

Exercise (for readers to attempt at the end of this topic followed by a group discussion):

- In your organization, how do employees prefer to engage each other? Do you think the choice of communication medium apt for the situations you have listed?

- From your work experience, come out with the positive experiences that face-to-face meetings have brought forth. Would you have achieved the same results if the same meeting was held over a telephone or instant messaging?

- Sit together as a team. List out all your meetings. Categorize the meetings as routine, priority, and discretional. Then, map it to the medium you want to employ—face-to-face or telephonic.

- Have you experienced a situation where you received an e-mail but a face-to-face communication would have meant so much better?

Types of face-to-face communication opportunities

Not all face-to-face interactions are sewn from the same cloth. One-to-one meetings, group meetings, and conferences are the popular ones, which are explained in detail here:

➤ **One-to-one informal**: These are the face-to-face interactions that happen outside the ambit of a company's governance structure. It is generally an ad hoc meeting called by any of the involved parties. A quick discussion about the roles and responsibilities with the manager and discussing technical topics between peers count towards informal meetings. In this type, you would generally be unprepared and the meeting happens on the fly. But when you are aware that the meeting is going to take place, think about all the possibilities, all the queries that could be raised, all the possible scenarios on why the meeting could be called in the limited amount of time given to you. The idea behind this tip is that you should never be unprepared heading into a meeting.

➤ **One-to-one formal**: These are the opposite of the informal meetings, mandated by the company's policies. Appraisals and skip-level meetings are some classic examples. In these meetings, the agenda is established well before the schedule date and time. You are required to prepare well in advance, and plan the discussion topics you want to bring up during this meeting.

➤ **Group meetings**: Similar to one-to-one formal meetings, this is a scheduled meeting, and consists of multiple participants. It has a well-established agenda, the goals to be achieved during the meeting, and picking up the action items from the previous meetings.

> **Seminars and conferences**: In this face-to-face communication, you generally have a single speaker addressing a fairly large group of people. The speaker is the main element of this communication, and needs to prepare the speech well in advance, practice delivering it, and time it accordingly. Further, the speaker needs to anticipate questions from the crowd and come up with the possible answers. This is a challenging form of face-to-face interaction as the various shades of listeners take in your message and interpret them differently.

> **Virtual face-to-face meetings**: Video conferences are an output of the advancement in technology and the extension of face-to-face communication, where the budgetary and time constraints are taken care of. All the rules of physical face-to-face communication apply to the virtual world as well.

Other types of face-to-face communication opportunities include trainings, debates, and role play.

Meetings

Meetings are an important part and parcel of IT professionals. Most of our communication takes place within the four walls of a meeting room. The objective of meetings is to achieve intended outcomes, and to achieve it communication is key. To state plainly, a meeting room is a place where information exchanges happen between participants at a rapid pace, with the intention to reach desired goals.

All meetings can be broken down into three sections:

> Preparation
> The actual meeting
> Post-meeting expectations

All three parts of the meeting are equally important whether you are attending or chairing it. We will delve into the three parts from a communication standpoint alone. I will not get into the nitty gritties of meetings, such as booking a conference room and ensuring a projector is in place, but will take you on a journey that necessitates the direct impact communication has on the objectives to be achieved.

There are a number of meetings that we come across in the IT world. Customer review, vendor selection, appraisal, and canteen committee meetings are a few examples.

Preparation

If you are calling for a meeting, then you are considered as a chairperson for the meeting. Here are various responsibilities of a meeting chairperson:

> ➤ Act as a facilitator who defines the agenda and lists out intended outcomes
>
> ➤ Identifies and invites required attendees
>
> ➤ Facilitates discussions and acts as a conduit for information to flow between attendees
>
> ➤ Formally communicates the ideas discussed and agreed during the meeting
>
> ➤ Circulates meeting notes (minutes of the meeting–MOM) after the meeting and reminds meeting attendees and stakeholders of the pending action items against them

If you are being invited to a meeting by the chairperson, then your role in the meeting would be an attendee or meeting participant. A meeting participant has responsibilities too in any meeting:

> ➤ Generate ideas for the topics on the agenda
>
> ➤ Play an active role in discussions aimed towards meeting the intended outcomes of the meeting
>
> ➤ Arrive at a solution, agree, or disagree on decisions to be made
>
> ➤ If there are any action items against the attendee, they need to duly completed before the deadline

Many attendees who I encounter in my IT life are of the opinion that they can just hop into a meeting sans preparation and participate as necessary. This is not ideal. This does not help them achieve the objectives of the meeting. You will not do justice to communicate effectively if you hope to recollect and brainstorm during the meeting. Brainstorming and thoughts pertaining to the agenda need to be played out before the meeting and during the meeting—brought forth and discussed.

The life of a chairperson is a little more elaborate before the meeting begins. First, the possible outcome of a meeting must be envisioned. For example, the objective is *selection of a new vendor for providing Internet connectivity*. Based on the objective, an agenda is put together by the chairperson and optionally reviewed by a peer or manager before finalizing. Based on the agenda, attendees must be identified and invited well in advance, and the agenda must be clearly communicated—along with any special preparation as needed. Every attendee must have a valid reason to be a part of the meeting and be active in discussions and provide good judgment. We don't need spectators around. Remember that communication is effective when the number of channels is fewer, and the more you add, the more muddled it becomes. And, you won't be doing yourself any justice by wasting participants' time.

To reiterate, a meeting room will witness plenty of communication exchanges. The pace is so rapid that the exchanges muddles your thinking. You may not be able to think on your feet as you would in the quietness of your cubicle or cabin. So, it is imperative that preparation in based on the circulated agenda is paramount. This translates into the agenda being well defined and crafted, which would be a key performance indicator for the meeting chairperson.

An agenda for a vendor selection meeting could look something like this:

1. Discuss individual vendors who participated in the tender process

2. Technical evaluation

3. Financial evaluation

4. Vendor selection

Never run meetings without the aid of slides. The chairperson is accountable for getting the presentation ready and reviewed before the meeting commences. The *Pillar 3 – slide preparation* section in *Chapter 7, Showcasing and Presentation*, will provide tips on how you can prepare effective slides.

Action Point

Exercise (for students to attempt at the end of this topic followed by a group discussion):

- Discuss whether you are going into meetings with or without preparations. Think objectively and share your opinions about whether the meetings you attend would have benefitted through proper preparations.

- If you are the chairperson, share your thoughts on how the meetings would have progressed if all participants had prepared before entering the meeting room.

- What is the process that your team/organization undertakes in preparing the agenda and choosing the list of attendees? Does it follow the process that I have listed?

The actual meeting

A chairperson is the leader of the meeting. The chairperson will facilitate discussions, allow all participants to share their views, channel the meeting towards desired outcomes, resolve conflicts, help build consensus on decisions, and ensure all attendees are aware of the decisions made during the meeting and the actions to undertake outside the confines of the meeting room.

On the other hand, participants come in fully prepared for the meeting. They will know exactly what they are going to share, and how they are going to proceed. As I mentioned earlier, no one should come into a meeting without preparation.

During the meetings, the chairperson would delegate the responsibility of minute taking to a colleague. The chairperson must concentrate on running the meeting and the notes coming out of the meeting must be taken up by somebody else who isn't an active participant in the discussions, but somebody who is knowledgeable enough to understand what is being talked about.

The opening

The onus is clearly on the chairperson on how the meeting breaks the ice. The chairperson must start the meeting by clearly stating the agenda, the possible outcomes that must be achieved before the meeting completes, and facilitate the introduction of participants. Getting started in a meeting is all about the energy levels and the chairperson must ensure that they set the right level of energy and ensure that every participant feels an innate part of it.

There are many other ground rules that meetings adhere to, but the critical one from a communication standpoint is that at any given point in time, only one person can speak. This will help in listening to what the attendee has to say before coming out with questions and countermeasures.

Action Point

Exercise (for students to attempt at the end of this topic followed by a group discussion):

- Run a mock meeting just to get the opening right. Let every team member get a chance to play chairperson and open the meeting. The manager can offer feedback based on team members' performance in the opening act.

The discussions

The reason why you are meeting today is that you have goals to accomplish. To accomplish listed goals, you need prudent information based on knowledge and experience, and the information sought is within the meeting room–participants are the source of this information. Every participant has a number of ideas—good, moderate, and bad for the situation. What is needed is to extract the good ideas, channel them towards meeting objectives, and agree with other meeting participants if the lead is solid. To do this, you need a facilitator who can lead the discussions, ask the right questions, remove clutter, and work on getting consensus for good ideas. This person is the chairperson of this meeting.

There are a number of ways to lead discussions. There is no right or wrong way of leading discussions. One of the ways is to ask questions—mainly open-ended questions to participants, encourage participation, and start playing devil's advocate to elaborate on the discussion of ideas generated. If you invoked certain ideas from a participant, ask others what they think about this and let them come out with their deductions and opinions. This will help bring in more minds to work on one idea at a time and choose the best idea available.

Rookie chairpersons are known to jump to a conclusion as soon as they see one. This is not healthy. Extract as many ideas as you can get out of the meeting, evaluate every single one of them, and pick the best one. Remember that the outcome of the meeting is not to generate an idea that fits the situation but to come out with the best option that is most productive to the team, organization, or client.

Take a look at the sample agenda provided in the *Preparation* section. The chairperson will introduce all the contenders vying for contract with your organization, which is the first part of the agenda. Next, every contender will be evaluated technically. The questions could be something like this:

➤ What do you think about the solution provided by vendor A?

➤ Why do you think this solution would work for us?

➤ Is there something more secure than what is offered by vendor C?

➤ What kind of experience do vendors A, C, and D have that fits the bill of our requirement?

You get the hint, right?

While the discussions are underway, a number of things could happen. The participant could start feeling the strain of the meeting and could show off uneasiness. Remember to announce break times well in advance, and stick to them as much as possible. Our minds work best with sufficient breaks in between.

It is common to see two or more participants might start having a mini conference among themselves and in the process distract the group and more importantly valuable ideas are going unheard by all present. Bring the participants back to the mainfold by asking them to share with the entire group. Do not allow mini conferences by establishing ground rules in advance.

Meetings generate a number of ideas. There are some that repel, and the participants could end up arguing by establishing that their idea is superior over the other. This leads to ego clashes, and hence conflicts. Conflicts based on egos are not good for information exchanges as they do not provide resistance-free channels for messages to pass through efficiently. The meeting leader must step in and resolve the conflict rather than let the participants burn each other verbally. The topic on conflict resolution is discussed later in this chapter.

Action Point

Exercise (for students to attempt at the end of this topic followed by a group discussion):

■ Another mock meeting. You are sitting in a meeting room to recommend the kind of smartphones that your organization must use. You have two choices—smartphones with Android or iOS operating systems. Divide the group into two while the manager plays chairperson. Let the discussions begin, and keep in mind all the tips that I have shared for fruitful outcomes to happen.

Closure

Meetings are efficient if they end on time with all the meeting objectives achieved. This is a rarity in IT, but there is always hope. Hence, we book back-to-back meetings on our schedule and the hope of meetings ending on time exists, doesn't it?

The closure part of the meeting does not have to end abruptly or skipped for the sake of time because discussions took longer than expected. Meeting closures are as important as the opening and discussion bit, so do not compromise this. Give it a sufficient length of time.

So how exactly do you close a meeting? Typically, the meeting chairperson would close the meeting by summarizing all the topics discussed and the action items that were agreed upon. Some topics that perhaps are not a part of the agenda will be picked up during the meeting. It is absolutely necessary in the interest of time and goal of achieving the agenda objectives to park such topics for a different meeting altogether. The chair would announce the date and time for a follow-up meeting if any. And lastly, all the attendees need to be thanked for actively participating in the meeting. This is most necessary as you command respect by making attendees feel important for their time and presence.

Post-meeting

The chairperson publishes the meeting minutes to all participants and other stakeholders who would be directly responsible for the outcome of this meeting. Be sure to ask the participants to vet the minutes' document for accuracy of topics discussed and decisions made. Remember that action items are tagged to a person, preferably who was in the meeting along with a target completion date.

Also announce the date and time of the follow-up meeting. It is also a good practice to ask for feedback from the attendees on how the meeting was run, whether the time was utilized well, and whether the focus centered on the agenda. Feedback is the breakfast of champions and as I discussed in *Chapter 2, From Governance to Communication*, it is essential for communication excellence. Meeting chairs can use the feedback comments to become better as well. Preparing minutes of the meeting including an example with a template is included in *Chapter 7, Showcasing and Presentation.*

Action Point

Exercise (for students to attempt at the end of this topic followed by a group discussion):

- For the mock discussion you conducted earlier, prepare minutes of the meeting (MOM) and what was discussed as a group to ensure all the important information is captured and how the action items were identified and recorded.

Nonverbal communication – body language

You may be sitting in a meeting and presenting all the wonderful things that your team has done, but with a drooped shoulder and hands below your waist; the content is getting across but the message is not. People read nonverbal signs, and trust it more than what the mouth has to say. Body language denotes various nonverbal forms of communication such as body gestures, hand movements, lip movements, facial expression, and eye contact among others.

Body language cuts across language and has hence grown to prominence owing to the subconscious signals the body emanates. For example, across languages and cultures, the nodding of a head from side to side means no and nodding vertically denotes acceptance.

Body language is a major area of study. In this book, I will touch base on aspects of body language that render communication effective and productive.

Breathing

Proper breathing leads to a healthy body. A healthy body exudes energy and energy reflects positive nonverbal communication. It is imperative that each one of us learn the way to breathe in order to send out the right signals from our bodies.

We all breathe. We do not think about breathing, it happens involuntarily. Nobody taught us how to breathe. It happened on its own just like the way we ate and set our first steps. But there is a problem, which off late has escalated to dangerous levels. The polluted air we breathe in lacks oxygen that our body requires to keep us in good fit. So, it is necessary for us to learn to breathe the right way and make it a habit so that our bodies can take over the process of the right way of breathing.

The art of breathing is extensively studied and put forth in yogic discipline called as *pranayama*. I have used the core principles of it and presented in this section.

The science behind breathing

Our body requires oxygen to keep all the functions running and alive. The amount of oxygen we take in has a major say in how we speak, how we move about, how we express with our face and how we think. Basically, everything we do (and don't do) are dependent on the oxygen intake.

Say that you are breathing, with inhalations at a very fast pace (shallow) which is how most people breathe. Carbon dioxide rises in your body due to shallow breathing. But your brain does not know it. It thinks that there is excess of oxygen as you are breathing well enough. This contradiction between what the brain thinks and what is available leads to stress and other related ill effects such as tiresomeness, distress, and panic. When you are under this cloud, you stop doing the right things, you stop moving the right way, your body starts to show the unease, and people around you are able to see it. If you are in a meeting communicating the wonderful things your team has achieved with this frame of body, you can probably assume what the audience will assume seeing one thing and listening to something else.

Breathing right

The objective of breathing is to inhale good amounts of oxygen that can be utilized by your body in producing energy. To take in higher amounts of oxygen, you need to breathe deep. Here is how you can do it the right way.

Sit straight while you do this. Breathing in must be through your nose. As you breathe in, take in air into your lower belly by physically expanding your stomach. As your lower belly reaches its limit, the upper belly area takes in oxygen. Once the upper belly is full, your chest takes in air.

Exhalation works on the concept of first in first out (FIFO). First, the air in your chest comes out followed by upper and lower abdomens. Breathing out is from your mouth. While you breathe out, push your belly in to rid of all the air.

You need to carry out this exercise daily whenever you find time—at the office or at home, especially before you chair meetings or a part of communication activities. As you practice it on a regular basis, the process of breathing right becomes involuntary and you will start breathing in the right way.

Pranayama teachers recommend that you breathe in X seconds, retain the air for 4X seconds and breathe out 2X seconds for best results. If we give a value of 5 to X, we would be breathing in through our nose for 5 seconds, retaining the air for 20 seconds and exhaling from our mouths for 10 seconds. Retaining the air for a longer duration ensures that the oxygen that is in our system is well absorbed by our body.

Action Point

Exercise (for students to attempt at the end of this topic followed by a group discussion):

- Let's test your photography skills. Think of how you want a portrait of yours be taken against the most amazing backdrop that you can imagine. First, do this while you breathe in oxygen. Write down what you saw. Next, think again while breathing out. You will experience that creativity is not at its best when you expire but is colorful and alive when you breathe in. This is a small indicator that breathing in brings richness to whatever activity you indulge in, creativity or not.

Posture

In ancient Zen and Yoga, it is said that the body attains balance in the area around the navel (belly button) in conjunction with hands. You will probably see Buddhist and Hindu monks keep their hands in this area while they meditate, and there is a reason for this. Not only the ancient teaching, but the modern workout regime considers the navel area critical. The stomach region is referred to as core in the workout dictionary. And, it is targeted to bring it to shape before concentrating on other parts of the body.

Notice any of the famous speakers around the globe and leaders who charm, their hands are majorly placed at a height where their navels are located. This is not coincidence but the realization of where the body's balance lies.

The communication posture

Posture makes a world of difference in communication too. If you have the right posture, people believe in you and trust the words that come out of your mouth. A person speaking with hands in his trouser pockets is less likely to be trusted over a person with hands in the tummy area.

Start observing people who are great orators and leaders, and see where their hands are. They are always above the waist, and at times go up to the chest height and come back down eventually to where the navel is.

You can try this out too. It applies not only during the communication act but also when you are standing still, watching a movie, or listening intently to a seminar speaker. You will feel your feet firmly attached to the ground you stand when your hands are in the close vicinity of your belly button.

In IT, most of us attend meetings where we are required to be in a seated position. Here too, you can practice the right posture. Don't sit too close to the table; instead, move a little away from it. Let your hands rest on your tummy or close to it. Avoid keeping your hands on the table or folding them. When people see your hands folded it sends out a signal that you are coming across aggressive. But having your hands around your tummy region gives you a virtual halo that makes you more accepting, trustworthy, and sincere.

If you are a speaker in a conference, avoid podiums. Step away from it if you are able to. Your hands get buried in it even if you are doing it right. People need to see the right signals from you and for that to happen, they need to see your hands operate, and operate in the region that radiates confidence.

Earlier is referred to leaders raising their hands chest high. Moving your hands to chest height is an indication of the energy you are building up and the passion you are putting through in the message. When you raise your hands chest high, your breathing picks up pace and you start building up energy. Hands at chest height must be used sparingly when you need to drive a point but it must always come back to the balanced position. If you stay at the chest high position for long periods of time, you start sounding like the pushy salesmen and after a while, you start to lose control over your words followed by sapping of energy levels.

You may also find speakers raising their hands over their heads to make a point. This is over aggression in getting the point across, and is not necessary in the field of IT. Perhaps in politics or a social cause, it may make sense!

Action Point

Exercise (for students to attempt at the end of this topic followed by a group discussion):

- Prepare a mini speech on your achievements that individuals of the team are going to deliver in front of the group. First, let the message be delivered with hands below the waist. Next, the same message with hands in the area around the navel.

> How did the speaker feel between the two versions? Which one brought in confidence and comfort?

> Did the listeners connect with the speaker with their hands below their waist or over?

Action Point

The expected outcome is that the speaker felt a lot more confident while they delivered the speech with their hands in the navel area and the listeners felt connected to words in this posture as well, and not so much with the former.

Proxemics

I introduced the concept of proxemics in *Chapter 2, From Governance to Communication*. It involves the physical spatial difference between the communicator and the listener. In face-to-face communication, proxemics play a critical role in getting the message across.

Humans are animals by evolution and we have instincts that make us possessive of the things that we hold control over. For example, if a colleague comes too close to your laptop, a distress signal hits your brain and you start to feel uncomfortable. You may not have marked your territory with urine as animals do but all of us have an imaginary periphery that we consider ours. Likewise, if a friend sits on a chair designated to you or leans across the vending machine that caters to you, you start feeling at ill ease, and aggression instincts take over. You will not accept this person into your circle of influence, or in other words, you will not heed to what this person communicates as the rapport takes a hit.

Be aware that people are possessive and respect their possessions by not intimidating them through physical proximity. Maintain a safe distance from people's possessions even if they are procured by the organizations. Also, when you speak to people who are sitting and you are in a standing position, this posture comes off as aggressive where you are looking down upon them. Try to avoid these situations.

On the other hand, as people get spatially closer to one another, their circles of influence over the other increases. Suppose I am sharing a new topic with you from ten feet, and then I move closer to you by five feet and continue sharing what I was sharing earlier. The influence I have over you, or the message that I am conveying gets across much more efficiently if the distance is lesser.

So how close can I get? If I get too close to you, you will start feeling awkward and start getting ideas other than the message that I am verbally stating. The general rule of thumb is that to communicate effectively, the audience must be able to see both your hands clearly. As long as they are able to see your hands, the closer you get to them, the better.

Edward T. Hall, the person who came up with the concept of proxemics, has defined various spaces depending on proximity. Intimate distance is between 0 and 18 inches, personal distance is 18 inches to four feet, social distance is four to ten feet, and public distance is from ten feet and beyond. However, these distances could be argued as they vary for people from different cultures. As I mentioned earlier, go with the hands rule and you should be just fine.

The handshake

In the business world, handshakes are the way of greeting, unless of course you are doing business with the Arab countries. A nice firm handshake is like setting things in motion for building rapport and effective communication. But, did you know that while you shake the hand of the other, there are a number of meanings that could be interpreted and read into depending on the way you shake it.

Some people just offer the hand as though a lady offers it for a kiss on the knuckle. They don't make an effort to hold the other person's hand or shake it. This kind of a handshake sends out the wrong message, and it does not exude confidence. Even before the meeting begins, such a handshake starts withering away the possible effective information exchanges.

On the other side of the spectrum, there are bone crushers. Their shakes are so firm that you start to remember the movie *Superman II* where Superman crunches Zod's hand while kneeling. Such shakes show off aggressive behavior and most don't appreciate it, especially if they are wearing rings with sharp edges!

A good handshake must be firm but must not intrude on the personal space of the other person. The pressure applied must not be soft, but not too hard either. That is not all; there is more to the firm handshake than you like to believe. When you do the shake, if you turn your hand over slightly so that your palm comes on top, you psychologically get an upper hand over the person shaking yours. On the other hand, if your hand turns slightly downward with your palm facing the ground, the other person will have an upper hand over you. So which technique should you use?

You can use both these handshakes for your advantage depending on the situation. If you are entering a negotiation with a vendor, it is always necessary to stand at a higher ground. To get this vantage point, when you shake, use the palms on top handshake. On the other hand, if you want to build a rapport with a fellow employee or gel with your boss, use the palm facing ground handshake. In principle, the upper handshake lowers the status of the other party, and in situations where you need the edge, go for it. The lower handshake makes the other person accepting of you and comfortable communicating with you.

Facial expressions

Just as pictures speak louder than words, the face expresses everything that you want to say, and everything that you want to keep it to yourself. In other words, our face reflects our moods more accurately than the verbiage and listeners look for the telltale signs that gives away the real you.

Masking your facial emotions to hide true feelings is an art. Poker players do it, hence the name that goes with the game—poker face. Even if they are staring at a royal flush, they put on a lifeless face that gives away absolutely nothing. Well, some take the help of props such as a hat for hiding eyebrow signs and dark sunglasses for the eye swelling possibly caused due to lack of sleep.

We are going to look at facial expressions from an aspect of putting on a face that goes with the message rather than reading facial expressions.

Facial expressions

Facial expressions bring out the real you and project your feelings onto your face. This is what we are designed to do. So, why did I bring up this topic? Did I bring this up to tell you to hide your true feelings and show your listener that all is happy and wonderful? Absolutely not!

The true essence of facial expressions is to give weightage to what you are speaking. If you are stating that you like a candidate to be brought onboard, show it in your face. Use the face to reinforce the message not only during positive conversations, but use it when you are disappointed with a colleague as well. Show them how disappointed you are with their performance and how this is impacting the organization. Whatever the kind of message may be, support it with your face and the listener will know full well that you are not messing around.

The next time you feel that you are not being perceived as you should be, take a look at your facial expressions and you will have the answers.

It all begins with the lips

You might be surprised to read this. The most important part of facial expressions is your mouth. Your mouth (read: lips) indicates a number of thoughts that runs through your mind. Some people have the habit of covering their mouth area while they speak, which is an annoying habit. Some people like to cover it to hide emotions. It is okay to cover it while you are yawning or coughing but not otherwise. In fact, do not cover your chin area as well. Many people like to read lips while they listen in, and you would be unobtrusively hindering the communication process.

Mona Lisa's smile has puzzled millions for centuries. She is portraying happiness and seriousness, all at the same time. Leonardo Da Vinci wanted to create dynamic expressions according to his memoirs. If you want to engage your listeners, put on the Mona Lisa smile. It invites audience to listen to you. And you are not showing all your cards at once; you hold back information and reveal it across your entire speech. If you have a face that says all is well, people listening will know how the message will flow and might not be fully engrossed in what you have to say.

People bite their lower lips when they have residual worries hovering about or when they are stressed. If you are speaking and biting your lower lip, do you think your listeners would get the right message? If you are listening in while biting your lips, do you think the speaker believes you to be a keen listener? You know the answer. Consciously avoid biting your lips, and this can have a reverse effect on your mind from wandering away to places. Likewise, people purse their lips as they have waves of suspicions hovering in their minds. Be conscious about what your lips are doing, and if you can stop your lips from pursing, it can help you avoiding being judgmental. You could always take a call on what is right and wrong after you have heard it all.

Show interest

In IT, communication can be cut and dry. It gets worse if the audience is not keen on the topic. What motivation will the speaker have if the audience is attending not on their own accord but through pressure from their managers, and are disinterested in what is being said? And, more importantly, every single communication session is valuable to the organization and from the organization standpoint they want to make every session count. So, from all these angles, it is only prudent that you show some interest.

Well, you can start by tilting your head to any one side slightly, which indicates that you are indeed listening. Follow this up with eyebrows raised slightly that respect the speaker and the words. And, the eyes; let them open up as well. Look at the speaker in the eyes, which further indicates that you are hearing the words. If you can do a combination of these three acts, the interest you are revealing will not just be shown off visually, but you start listening in as well. On a related note, if you are staring at anything other than the eyes of the speaker or the presentation on the screen, you are gravely expressing to the speaker that you disinterested in the session. Avoid it at all costs. Your time is limited. While you are physically in a session, stay mentally present as well. You will end up making the best use of your time.

Some people nod their heads in the vertical plan to tell the speaker nonverbally that you are not just hearing the words but listening to it. The nod also tells oneself that the message is sinking in, and there is an agreement with what is being heard. It is one of the ways to understand what is being said and showing interest but when overdone, it can mean other things as well. A steady nod means that I am listening and a fast one done vigorously indicates that you are ready to be done with the speaker. You are showing impatience by nonverbally asking the speaker to close the topic.

Action Point

Exercise (for students to attempt at the end of this topic followed by a group discussion):

- The next time you are in a meeting or a seminar, ask your colleagues to observe you for a few minutes to understand what your facial expressions are revealing. Compare this with what was actually going on in your mind. For example, if you are listening to a technical talk that you are disinterested in, it is but natural for you to look at your watch, at people around you, and do everything else other than nodding or raising your eyebrows. Now what is going on inside your head and what you are facially indicating match.

- Now in the same meeting, express your interest by tilting your head slightly, raising your eyebrows and make eye contact with the speaker. Notice the difference of how you are taking in information compared to before.

- It is a fact that all of us spend more time with our colleagues than family. We know the mannerisms and habits of one another quite well. Sit in a circle, and be candid about how each of your express your emotions through your face, and what your thoughts are around it. It is fair to say that we may not know how we are expressing visually, and we need the feedback to orient us the right way.

Conflict management

We are humans and conflicts are an inherent part of who we are. Conflicts happen and there is no way of getting around it. We must deal with them when they come about and turn them into an advantage. I will talk about how we can do it a little later.

There are a number of causes for why people conflict in the first place. The prime reason is communication failure. People misunderstand each other, misunderstand the words spoken and misunderstand those that aren't. If we get around to plugging the miscommunication factor, we can live in a conflict-free world. Do you think that can happen? Unfortunately, never. But, we can reduce a good percentage of workplace conflicts.

Apart from communication failure, conflicts are caused due to personality traits. Each person is unique in their own ways. Some personalities get along with others while others don't. This is how we are, and there is no elixir that can ebb it from its root. The only way to deal with conflicts evolving from personalities is to accept others as they are and move on with what we do. In this book, I will concentrate on communication-related conflicts and not get into personality-related ones.

Conflicts arising out of communication

We communicate with each other in analog signals. It would help if it was digital, where the possibility is between 0 or 1. Each one of us think, feel, and act differently, and this can bring about a number of permutations and combinations for coming up with conflicts. *My boss asked me to get this done, but he did not ask but ordered me to do it. I am in an IT job and not in a prison where you do as you are told.* See how conflicts can happen, how trivial issues can blow up and could avalanche their way into blowing things out of proportion. Perhaps the boss had a gun to his head, and wanted this task to be done on priority without exceptions. Or this is the way the boss communicates with everybody. Either way, the problem is communication. If and only if the boss had explained the need for the task to be done on time, and explained the situation, the conflict would have never arisen.

Here are some causes of conflicts that arise from communication breakdown:

> **The way people communicate**: Everybody is different. This applies to the way they talk, express their feelings (or don't), and react to situations.

> **Difference of opinions**: When presented with a situation, people come up with their own ideas, solutions, and opinions. Some opinions complement one another while others repel. When peoples' opinions do not get along, we have a classic situation of a conflict on our hands.

> **Goals**: If every player on a soccer team does not aim to hit into the opposition's goal post, we have a conflict of interest. This happens in organizations often, and is perhaps a hard one to deal with.

> **Areas of responsibility**: To build a house, you need masons, carpenters, plumbers, and architects, among many other functional roles. Likewise, in an organization, employees play various roles. Conflicts occur if employees are not privy to how their work contributes to the overall success of the organization and the lines of responsibility between theirs and others.

> **Setting expectations**: If bosses do not set the right expectations with their subordinates, or do not communicate what the expectations are, you are right, you have a brooding conflict.

> **Changes**: There is a popular saying that goes about in IT organizations that goes something like "change is the only constant". Changes are never good. We get used to certain way of working. If it is a beneficial change from an employee's perspective, there is acceptance, if not, we have a conflict on our hands.

Medium for conflict resolution

We have discussed various mediums so far for communication to happen—mainly written and face-to-face. Guess which one is best suited for resolving conflicts: face to face. If the conflicting parties are collocated, then consider resolving conflicts half done.

Having people sit across from one another brings out in entirety of who we are, whether we are genuinely sorry for something we have done or we are emotionally attached to the solution that we proposed. Whatever the conflict could be, if you can get people in the same room, opt for it. In today's world, physical proximity is a luxury but if it is available, don't look at any other medium.

Conflicts owing to communication styles

Flashback to *Chapter 1, Communication Training*, where I introduced the topic of various communication styles. We looked briefly at four distinct types of personalities who are either goal-oriented, people-oriented, solo workers, and data gatherers. Conflicts arise when people involved in communication do not understand the communication style of the other party, and set expectations from their perspective alone.

A little regard to what the other person is like would do a world of good in exchanging information without attached emotions—read possible conflicting situations.

Some people are straightforward. They tell you what they want and do not care for niceties. This might rub others the wrong way, and they start disliking the person, bitch about them behind their back and try to bring about their downfall. Do you know what the root causes of these ill effects are? It is not the communication style, it is ego. Our egos don't allow us to take things as they are. Our egoistic minds sets an imaginary bar in our minds, and anybody who doesn't come up to it are possible candidates for disliking and unfriendly behavior. If you want to stay happy, quash your egos. Personality-related conflicts can be cut down if egos are under check.

Think objectively and not subjectively

Conflict resolution must be about the objective that we are trying to achieve and not the persons involved.

Whenever there are conflicts arising out of decisions, ideas, and opinions, take a step back and understand what needs to be achieved rather than the people who are involved in making the decision. If you want to hire a new vendor, list down all the qualities that you would like from the vendor and start striking off those who don't make the cut. Instead, if you discuss vendors individually who are nominated by different managers, you are bound to escalate the situation by falling into the trap of me against you.

Conflicts are good. They are not always negative. When people oppose decisions and ideas, dirt comes out into the open, thereby allowing decision-makers to brainstorm and take the right decision.

Open communication for resolving and avoiding conflicts

Conflicts are present where transparency isn't. The sole source of majority of conflicts is a lack of transparency between the parties involved, and you could also read this as lack of communication.

If a manager is setting expectations from his subordinate, they are well within their right, but it is only fair that the subordinate knows and agrees with the expectations set. Ideally, a manager must set their expectations on paper first and then bring the subordinate into a meeting and explain what is to be done. The subordinate can digest the information and make a decision on whether to accept it or negotiate the activities assigned. It is not uncommon that expectations set by a manager are unrealistic. So, the subordinate would like to justify the reasons for not accepting the expectations.

The situation we have just discussed is a mere example to showcase how transparent communication can prevent possible conflicts. A manager and subordinate can communicate all that they want and arrive at a midway point that is acceptable to both. Let's say that a manager has set his expectations from his subordinates. The subordinates are left with no choice but to accept it with a pinch of salt. Even though the subordinate accepted it with a pinch of salt, a cold war would have brewed between them, which would eventually lead to conflicts, lack of productivity, absenteeism, and performance dip among a host of other undesirables.

Likewise, in organizations, where all decisions, changes, goal setting exercises, division of work, appraisals, and all other activities bring together multiple parties into the foray on the principle of open and transparent communication—with an aim to avoid possible conflicts. Yet, conflicts will arise, no matter how open and transparent the communication is. Even when you apply the principle, you will still have some conflicts coming out of it. Some parties might declare to *agree to disagree*. In those cases apply the tip on thinking objectively on what is needed to be achieved rather than the people involved.

Action Point

Exercise (for students to attempt at the end of this topic followed by a group discussion):

- As I mentioned in this chapter, there are workplace conflicts in all organizations and teams. Share the conflicts that you faced and how they were resolved. For the unresolved conflicts, apply the principles that I have shared to bring about closure.

Controlling face-to-face Interactions

When you are in a meeting, you ideally want to be in control of it and not the other way around it. You want to take the meeting as you wish to and bring up points that you want and in the order that you have set. If you are addressing your subordinates, you can confidently say that you can do it each and every time. What about meetings with customers? How sure are you? Not the same as it is with your subordinates, is it?

Leading and pacing is a technique that helps you take control over the face-to-face interaction you are in. You could sit as a mediator trying to resolve conflicts, or apprising your team of the changed goal sheet. One of the sure ways of getting their attention, getting people to take you seriously and to follow your lead, is through this technique.

The methodology works something like this. You start mirroring the person who you are interacting with. After you continue doing this for a while, the party who you are conversing will get a whiff of it, and starts to feel *in sync* with you. And then you can start leading the person by doing something else, and the person will follow you. Once you are in this zone, you can take control of the meeting, and start leading it your way.

Let me expand on this with an example.

Step 1 – Pacing

The people who you interact with do not sit idle. They have a certain posture, voice intonation, move their hands in a certain way, and have various distinctive mannerisms. Your first task is to observe the person. Identify one or two mannerisms that you can mime. Say the person has his arms crossed and speaks in a low pitch. How difficult is it to match these two? So you will start mimicking these two actions, and if the person changes his posture with arms on the table, you will do so.

Other items that you can mimic are breathing rate, head nods, verbiage, blink rate, and speech rate. While you do it, don't make it obvious. Let the pacing activity be subtle.

Step 2 – Locking

How long will you continue mirroring the person in front of you? As long as it takes for the sync to set in. You will know that the sync has happened when the person starts to mimic you after some time. You can test for the synchronous movements from time to time by moving your hands off the table and see whether the person does the same too.

The mimicking movements of the person across the table signifies that you have built a rapport at a subconscious level. Make sure that the people in the room never get a whiff of what you are doing. You would have built a sphere of influence that you can leverage on in the next step.

Step 3 – Leading

Now the sync has set in, it is time for you to make the moves. You can start by suggesting—"Why don't we discuss the new requirements?" The customer sitting across the room will oblige because the person can feel the *connection*. In this way, you run the face-to-face interaction as you would like as long as your suggestions are not ludicrous, such as "Why don't we go dancing?" If the connection is strong, then your customer may be up for this suggestion too!

Try the three steps out. It works. You need to take care of identifying mannerisms and mirror them subtly.

Suppose you have two people in the room. You can still mimic both of them together. If one of them has crossed his legs and the other has folded his arms do both the activities together. You are upping the bar by mirroring two people simultaneously. This will take time but practice it on one person.

Action Point

Exercise (for students to attempt at the end of this topic followed by a group discussion):

- For your organization, how important it is do you think that meetings, especially face to face, go according to plan?

- Run a mock session with two individuals. Let one mimic the other, and the person who is being mirrored share the experience of how the feeling was being mimicked and the possible connection that was felt.

- In another mock session, run all the three steps and see the results of improved connection and hence control over sessions through effective communication.

Summary

As this chapter ends, you are expected to know the following:

Understanding the importance of face-to-face communication and when to employ it

How to prepare, run, and close meetings

Basics of body language, more specifically concentrated on breathing, posture, physical proximity, and the right way to shake hands

Basics of facial expressions and how to show interest with the lips and the eyes

Introduction to conflict management, and tips for resolving conflicts in organizations

The principle of pacing and leading for controlling face-to-face interactions

In *Chapter 7, Showcasing and Presentation*, we will look at how your presentation skills can be improved thereby increasing your confidence during meetings, speaking assignments, and lectures. We will also look at preparing meaningful presentations and minutes of the meeting.

>7

Showcasing and Presentation

Presentation is typically formal communication where a speaker presents information, ideas, or new products in a group setting (to an audience, irrespective of the size). Presentations can take place in various contexts—seminars, webinars, or face-to-face meetings. It is a form of communication that can rake maximum effect and can be a powerful tool if used right. Likewise, it can bring downfall faster than the speed of light if things go haywire.

Presentations are not generic. A good presenter will not use the same presentation for all types of audience—be it using a particular presentation for IT professionals, medical practitioners, or civil servants. The presentation will have to be tweaked for the audience in question. The style of delivery too differs from one situation to another. The crux of a presentation becoming effective is to make it subjective. If not, even if it is delivered with full confidence and with enamoring style, it is still bound to fail. The objective is that the audience becomes (hopefully) knowledgeable about the topic, and this is possible only through effective presentation. In this chapter, I will present tips that can help you become a better presenter.

Importance of presentations for employees

Why are presentations important you might ask? My work should speak for itself and it doesn't need the sugar coating that presentations normally do, you argue. I would have agreed with you if you were the only employee working in the company with the customers, senior management, and the outside world focused on your deliverables, and nothing else. This probably happens in the dream world that we encounter in the middle of the night from time to time but not in the IT world. The competition is cut throat. Employees fight against the other employees over visibility, opportunities, and recognition. This kind of a world requires you to highlight your achievements in the least time possible—a reminder of the patience-stricken world we live in.

A good presentation does more than just highlight the achievements or the focus of your intended content. It builds rapport and relationship with the customers or whoever is sitting at the receiving end. I have previously discussed the importance of rapport and relationships in communication in *Chapter 2, From Governance to Communication*. Apart from the communication angle, relationships take you places—they bring in new projects, new customers, organizational movements, promotions, and so on.

To sum up, showcasing your achievements and yourself is the key factor to succeed. It requires as much (or maybe more) effort as you have put into developing your product or deliverable. Let showcasing and presentation of your delivery be taken into the sphere of activities that you perform so that you prepare, plan, and execute it effectively.

Four types of presentation

In line with the four types of written communication, presentations can be logically segregated into four distinct types, as shown in the following image:

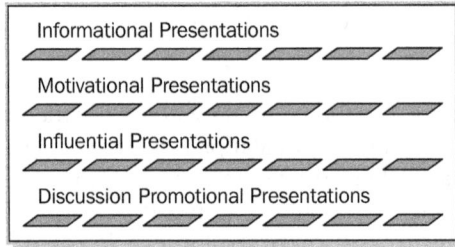

Informational presentations exist for the purpose of sharing information, and nothing more. Examples include company performance declaration and the news on TV. Presenters are required to communicate slowly and clearly. The flow of information must be logical and sequential, and questions are accepted for further clarification.

Motivational presentations are a different bunch. They exist for the sole purpose of changing an audience's state of mind into doing something constructive. There are a number of motivational speakers touring the world—Anthony Robbins, Brian Tracy, and Robert Kiyosaki to name a few. In fact, you or your manager could be playing the role of a motivator in your organization. It requires the presenter to be passionate and reasonable about the chosen topic, and at the end of the presentation, the audience must be on their toes to transform into a better person. The motivational presenter must also take in the negative views of the listeners and present a future that has rays of hope embedded within it.

Influential presentations are meant to persuade an audience into latching onto the idea presented. A classic example is that of a salesperson highlighting the positives of a product and the various benefits that behold the consumer. The presenter in this case must be grounded on facts, and must show trustworthiness. Apart from this, he or she must consider the views of the audience (read objections) into presenting the case or making a pitch. Other examples are political rallies and spiritual congregations.

The last type of presentation in vogue in IT organizations is the presentation that promotes discussions. This is perhaps critical in terms of value to the organization as a number of ideas are generated through brainstorming and probing. I have been part of discussions surrounding ways of cost cutbacks, performance appreciation, and other technical solution discussions. The presenter must simply throw open the topic with the known facts and not opinions. The idea is to scoop thoughts and opinions from the audience. The presenter must never reject any ideas on face value, and must welcome all the thoughts that come across.

In the next section, I will discuss the four essential pillars of presentation, and the things that the presenter must do to be effective.

Four pillars of presentation

Many people believe that good presentation is all about the oratory skills that the speaker possesses. This is so untrue. Oration is just a small element in the overall presentation framework. There is much more to presentation than the speaking skill itself.

Presenting is a work of art, an art that can be the factor for success or failure. There are five principles that I personally stick to during presentations. The principles are not comprehensive, but they work every single time, be it in an IT environment or not:

> ➤ Presentation must be about the audience and not the narcissist in you
> ➤ Connection with your audience is a must for presentations to be effective
> ➤ Good speaking skills help in presenting, but it is not the alpha and the omega
> ➤ Slides employed are a guide to remember topics but not a reading list
> ➤ Preparation is key for any presentation to work

If you break down the end-to-end activity of presentation, you can observe that there are basically four major aspects that you need to master in order get presentation right—every time. The four major aspects are the pillars that erect the presentation from the roots branching towards the sky. The following image lists the four pillars of presentation:

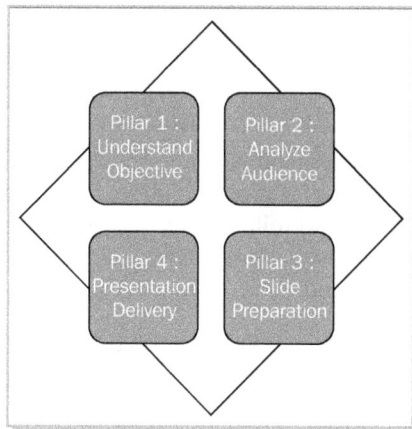

Pillar 1 – understanding the objective of the presentation

Why am I doing what I am doing? Why am I delivering this training to this group of IT personnel? What is the audience going to get out of this presentation?

These are some of the questions that you need to ask yourself before jumping onto slide preparation. The answers to similar questions will unravel the path to content preparation and subsequent presentation delivery. You may not always have the answers to these questions, but make sure you get answers from people who are cognizant of the underlying objective.

The entire exercise of coming up with such questions and seeking answers to them is aimed at understanding the objective. Everything we do, in IT and outside, circles around our motives and the objectives we want to achieve.

Let's pick up an example of training on a certain technical topic. What is the objective of the training that you are going to deliver?

➤ Is it to equip the team to be effective at work?

➤ Is it to support the team in appearing for a certification exam?

➤ Or both 1 and 2.

If you know the answer to the question, you are in a strong position to analyze your audience, prepare content, and deliver. Let's say that the answer is to support the team to appear for a certification exam. How differently would you prepare for the presentation? You would base the training around the needs of the exam, and include tips to answer the questions and cover the syllabus that the certification body prescribes. You may not give much thought to the work that the IT employees are performing nor bring up differences that exist in reality from what is mandated by the certification body.

Technique – pen on paper

Most people think well when they start to write down questions and start answering them on the same medium. The process helps us offload the probing questions from our mind and to think further on the objectives.

I am a *writing* person. I think well when I write things down. Sure, it slows me down, but I am as effective as I can be with pen and paper at my disposal. During my consulting sessions, I have coached a number of senior executives to follow this method to unload the various things on their minds and follow it up with prioritizing and rethinking on what needs to get achieved. It has produced great results. It is a simple two-step approach, and is as uncomplicated as a baby's mind:

➤ Articulate your objective as clearly as possible. For example, make bullet points like the following:

➤ Train employees of the team on the new features of the e-mail program

➤ Inform subordinates of the policy change in the organization

➤ Showcase organization's performance to the customer

➤ While you do this, you are getting your mind oriented towards what needs to be achieved and what should be covered. Just write down the question—why am I doing this? And then the objectives open up as clear as day.

➤ Now that you know what you need to achieve, sit in the position of the audience and think about what they would like to get out of this presentation. It is quite common in IT that a good portion of the audience in any meeting would be bored out of their minds as the content is irrelevant to them. So, in such cases, the presenter is perhaps thinking about a section of the audience and not the whole. If you need to be a great presenter, you need to take everybody into consideration and plan your presentation to cover everyone. We will come to the specifics as we move further in this chapter.

In this two-step process, we first focused on the objective from the presenter's standpoint and then expectations from the audience standpoint. This 360-degree view will give us the clarity to come up with powerful and effective presentations. Like I said earlier, presentation is not only about speaking, there is a lot more to it, and the following exercise will demonstrate this.

Action Point

Exercise (for readers to attempt at the end of this topic followed by a group discussion):

■ You have a number of meetings scheduled on your calendar. And, you may be chairing quite a few of them. If you are chairing them, for every meeting, write down the objectives from your standpoint and what you think the expectations from the audience will be. Once you come out with your observations, see how differently you would start presenting and how effective the whole process becomes.

Pillar 2 – analyzing the audience for the presentation

In the game of presenting, it is always preferable to choose horses for courses. Even before you start preparing your slides, you need to know your audience to be as effective as you can be; you need to put yourself in the audience's shoes—so that you can weave the fibers of connection, which is the entire essence of presentation. The chance of you appealing to the audience is much greater if you have analyzed your audience and prepared the presentation accordingly, don't you think? Imagine bringing up the topic of how Microsoft got the idea of GUI in a conference attended by Microsoft employees! You wouldn't exactly be connecting with the audience, instead repelling them from you.

My point being that audience analysis is absolutely necessary, important, and mandatory before you start preparing for presentations. It renders your time being used in the most effective manner as you relate the topics of the presentation and the style of delivery to the people who matter.

There is no right or wrong way to analyze the audience. Every presenter has a different way of analyzing audiences. When I train IT personnel, I send out a template which all participants have to fill out. I ask for the number of years of IT experience, domain expertise, prior knowledge on the subject, and their expectations from the course. This information will help me prepare better, scale up or scale down, provide domain-relevant examples, and better connect with the audience by meeting their expectations.

What are the other ways of doing it if you do not have the comfort of obtaining information or if you are facing a large group?

Try to gather demographic information such as age, the general domain of expertise, gender, and the geographical origin. If you have a good majority of folks listening who are from the southern states in America, they may not appreciate you cracking redneck jokes to highlight concepts. If the audience is mainly conservative, you may play safe by staying away from stating examples that are generally considered under the belt.

All I have done is give you examples. When you present, it is up to you to correlate the content with the demography of your audience, and alter the presentation based on these factors. Barack Obama based his presidential campaign on the theme of change as his campaign managers analyzed the mood of the voters who felt anger towards the fight against Iraq and the failing financial system.

Another school of thought tells us that a presenter must make the audience think, feel, and do. Presentation must go beyond just delivering information but rather make them think on the topic, connect emotionally to it, and get motivated to do something constructive. A good motivational speech has the power to make people think of the pleasure of doing great things, feel the pain that comes out of non-action, and work constructively towards pleasure and staying away from pain.

Action Point

Exercise (for readers to attempt at the end of this topic followed by a group discussion):

- You are delivering a presentation on why communication in English is important in offices, be it IT or non IT. Your audience is made up of native English speakers who have nominated themselves to this training. A quick check of your database reveals that most of them have not graduated from college. How will you go about presenting on this topic?

Pillar 3 – slide preparation

Presentations must have slides; even if it is not in the benefit of the presenter, the audience finds it easier to follow if there is a slide highlighting the various points being brought up. I am aware that some traditional presenters stay away from slides. I would advise against not using them; they are a necessity.

The real work towards getting your presentation on paper starts with the preparation of slides. The things that would be brought forth during the presentation are first brain dumped onto the slide and then spoken about during the presentation. It is important to note that slides must be used as a guide for presenters and the audience to follow and not as a reading material for the presenter. Slides must not contain everything there is to the presentation but rather pointers alone. If slides contain every word that will be spoken, perhaps there is no need for the fourth pillar, presentation delivery, to happen.

The three-step approach

There are three major steps that we need to imbibe to get slide preparation right:

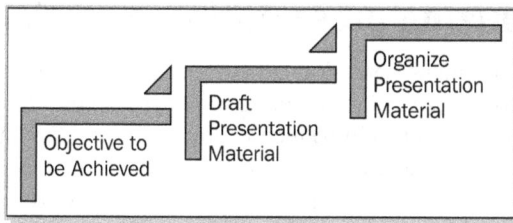

Step 1 – Objective to be achieved

Step 1 in preparing slides is a combination of pillar 1 and 2—understanding the objective of the presentation and analyzing the audience. Before you sit down to prepare slides, you need to know what you are trying to achieve and who you are aiming at. Unless you have answers to these two enigmas, you will not be in the best position to prepare effective slides, and that would reflect on the presentation being delivered.

Step 2 – Draft presentation material

Sounds straightforward doesn't it? Not really!

A presentation must have an outline. It is a framework that will help you connect your topics and provide synergy to achieve the objective of presentation. The outline must simply contain main topics and nothing else—no secondary content. After you get your outline draft as per your satisfaction, start filling in the secondary data that will make up your main topics. Remember that creation of an outline at the beginning does not make it a rigid one—meaning you cannot change the outline after it's frozen. You must modify your outline if the altered avatar provides a robust reinforcement to the presentation. The whole idea is that there must be a framework, and not bring in rigidity which sets rules which act like boundaries to work within.

In this step, you must not think about what comes after what, and at what position. Brainstorm and put your ideas on a sheet of paper. Write down all the things you want to cover as a part of the presentation. Start with brainstorming all the high-level items to begin with. And then dig one layer deeper, not necessarily concentrating on one main point after another, but rather whatever comes to your mind. Move back and forth as and when new thoughts flash across the topics of interest. The process must help you gather all that is in your mind and in your research quickly transferred to slides and aid you in not losing ideas.

Before I started writing this book, I created an outline with the chapter names and the brief content that went into each chapter. Once I was satisfied with the chapter outline, I started to expand on the individual topics that chapters would contain. This helped me focus my thoughts towards a wide horizon to start with and concentrate on the specifics as I went deeper into the structure. During the process of identifying topics within the chapters, I made some changes to the outline as well –a lot got revealed about the outline as I started to think deep on the individual topics. Did I freeze the outline at this point? No. Even during the writing process, the outline got changed to better accommodate like-minded topics—which I am going to discuss in the organizing step of this three-step process.

Step 3 – Organizing presentation material

As of step 2, you have all the presentation content in hand. You now have to move it around to give a flow to the presentation and to make your presentation sound like a story. For example, you probably want to introduce various concepts first, and then move into the specifics. From my experience, within the context of entire presentations, this is the part that gives me most pleasure—as it gives me the control over the presentation, what topics I want to bring at what juncture, and so on.

There are other ways of building a presentation which are in vogue but not ideal. Some people like to list one main topic, and think over the topic to come up with all the sub topics. Once this main topic is covered, they move over to the next and repeat the process. This may sound disciplined and uniform, but it does not help in the ideation process. Our thoughts don't work like a train where whenever a station approaches passengers designated for that station get off the train. Our minds are dynamic. They throw in a lot of ideas at any juncture in time. When I am in a seminar, I am simultaneously thinking of what blog post to write on, and what meetings I need to attend tomorrow, and so on. I cannot just sit and channel all my brain cells towards one object. Neither can you. This is how we are built. We need to use this dynamism to generate ideas, throw them around as and when we get them, and then sit calmly and organize. This may sound agnostic, but it is the natural process of generating ideas.

Action Point

Exercise (for readers to attempt at the end of this topic followed by a group discussion):

- Pick a topic that you have expertise over. It need not be related to IT at all. Pick anything like cooking, gardening, web design, or leadership. Discuss an objective that you want to achieve through your presentation, and prepare slides based on two processes:

  - A few in the group prepare slides using the brainstorming method.

  - The rest in the group use the linear approach of main points followed by sub points.

- When you are done preparing the presentation, discuss how the process felt in each of the cases and how the other process could have been better or worse.

Pillar 4 – presentation delivery

Pillar 4 is show time! Your entire preparation including understanding the objective, analyzing the audience, and preparing material is to materialize the delivery of your presentation, which perhaps requires the shortest period compared to other pillars. But, this is the activity that matters. It is this activity which will make or break the objectives you are about to achieve. Suppose you have done a great job in pillars 1, 2, and 3; you will have the greatest chance of succeeding in pillar 4. If you have faltered in one of the earlier pillars, you will have to depend on prayers rather than your ability to pass through the cracks. In short, all four pillars are important, although presentation delivery representing pillar 4 seems like the junction of salvation.

The secret behind good speakers

It is believed that good speakers make great presenters. It is true that you need to speak well to communicate effectively to the audience. But, guess what differentiates a good speaker from an ordinary one. Practice.

Good orators practice their skill over and over again before the show begins. My point being, everybody can be good at speaking if they put in the effort and practice hard at it. You need to run full-length rehearsals well before the presentation is scheduled. You need to master your body language when you express certain ideas, work on intonations for thoughts that are critical, and practice body movements—like keeping your hands around the area of your stomach and breathing deep.

If you have difficult sections in your presentation, rehearse them a number of times as long as it takes to make you confident. Put on the shoes of your audience to intuit the kind of questions that they might pose. Get ready with responses. Be as prepared as you can be.

Time your sessions. You don't want to fall behind or rush ahead. It will only add to the anxiety levels that you might be carrying before the session starts. During rehearsals, jot down the time you are consuming on each topic. Append some buffers for the questions that the audience might pose.

These are several ingredients that make a good speaker. Everyone can aspire to be one, and all it takes is effort and not innate talent.

Controlling nerves

You might think that fresh presenters have a problem with controlling their anxiety levels before the presentation begins. Wrong! Yes, they feel the nerves, but so do the experienced ones. All good and confident speakers feel a tinge of anxiety before you start to speak and up until a point where you feel you have adjusted to the new environment and the flow has set in.

Regarding the anxiety levels, it is not about having them, but rather being in control of them. This is the difference between good speakers and others. Good speakers, with practice behind their backs, will have some anxiety to start with, but through their confidence coming out of backbreaking preparation they are able to control it. If a presenter has not practiced, then he or she might feel it is hard to control their nerves as there are likely to be topics that are relatively alien to the presenter as they are to the audience. Probably, the presenter does not know what he or she needs to cite, and what kind of questions may be posed to them.

If a presenter does not feel a rise in anxiety levels before the presentation is due to begin, either the speaker is overconfident or does not care a damn about the outcome of the presentation. Both cases are not beneficial. Overconfidence signifies egotistic behavior and it can have repercussions in looking down upon the audience, and if the speaker does not care about what the audience thinks about the presentation, it is likely that there would be minimal feedback and the outcome of the feedback will have no impact on the speaker. Throughout this book, I have been stressing on the importance of feedback, and overconfidence and narcissism could overthrow the essence on which these principles are built upon.

On the other side of the spectrum, we have speakers who are irrationally nervous. There is no reason to their madness. Presenters who I have spoken to have various reasons for their increasing levels of anxiety. The audience not liking the face and style of the speaker, the speaker forgetting the words and the examples during the show, and the speaker finishing early without sufficient material to go through to the end are some insane reasons for the rising anxiety levels. My answer is simple, and I am repeating what I have stated earlier. If there is sufficient practice before the presentation, there is no reason to be irrationally nervous. If you have prepared well across all pillars, there is no reason why the audience will find reasons to hate you. Remember that the audience is listening to you because they want to benefit and not to find reasons to put you down. They want you to succeed, and that is the only way they are going to get anything solid from the presentation and the time they have invested.

To summarize, some amount of anxiety is good, as long as it is under control. Don't get overconfident or irrationally nervous.

Get familiar with technology

Jesus preached the Sermon on the Mount on a hilltop next to the Sea of Galilee. He did not have any props or any material that he used to deliver the sermon. In our case, it is quite different. We have a number of aids, namely an overhead projector, motorized white screens, wireless connections to the projector, lighting, laser guns, and many more. While we master the presentation delivery, body language, intonation, and breathing, we must also get familiarized with the technology that we leverage upon.

We need to invariably get accustomed to every gadget that we employ. We don't have a choice these days to have assistants to take care of technological aspects. The presenter must be an all-rounder!

What happens if the speaker is not aware of all the gadgets that he or she employs and requires help from some of the audience or other staff to get it to work right? Well, speakers work on a rhythm that helps them in the flow while they present. If the presenter has to pause, take help, and then move on, the rhythm is broken and the distraction would have caused irreparable damage to the flow and to confidence levels.

Secondly, whenever help is sought, it eats into the time of the presentation. This leads to unnecessary delays, and once again comes back to haunt the presenter to finish the presentation on time—meaning they rush through the topics, which can upset the effectiveness of the communication and the flow.

My advice is simple. Find out all the gadgets that you are going to use. Get familiarized with them. If you can visit the conference room and connect your laptop to make sure it works fine, it would be the icing on the cake in regards to the preparation you have made.

Action Point

Exercise (for readers to attempt at the end of this topic followed by a group discussion):

- You have a presentation that is prepared from the last exercise. Now, present it after sufficient practice and make time estimates.

- Take a moment for self-feedback on your levels of anxiety and the kind of thoughts that were running through your mind. How did you control your nerves if you did so? Share this with the group. Let the audience provide feedback on what they saw in you—whether they saw a confident speaker who was well versed with the material or somebody who was taken over by nerves.

Creating content for effective presentations

You need to create quality content to effectively communicate the subject matter. There are no set rules to prepare slides. Everybody comes up with their own or copy from their peers without giving much thought to how the content would look from the receiving end. Yes, it should go without saying that you create content that the audience can follow rather than a presentation which is comfortable for you to present.

By the time you create content, you would have got a handle on the objectives you have to achieve and would have a good idea of who your audience is. So creating content with these two pillar stones in place is like including the necessary nutrients and removing the flab from the meat. And do it from the perspective of the audience—meaning a logical flow that the audience are able to follow and connect the dots.

Traditional content

Although IT has not existed forever, there are paradigms that are involuntarily set up and which are still in vogue. One of them is the presentation content. A typical presentation in an IT organization will consist of the following topics:

1. Title page
2. Agenda
3. Introduction
4. Topic 1
5. Topic 2, Topic 3, and so on
6. Questions
7. Thank you slide

This flow works. It has worked for a long time and it will continue to exist. You basically set the agenda, introduce the topics, and go through them. How can it not work? There is a flow that the presenter can run through. Take up one topic at a time and progress gradually to the end. This sounds very presenter oriented rather than focused on the audience. Can the audience grab one topic after another? Is it a sequential way of presenting that matches how our brains work in grasping information? Remember, the objective is not to run through the slides from start to finish, but to ensure that the audience gets what is presented. So, it must be vetted from the perspective of the audience.

I mentioned earlier that the traditional way of presenting content has worked for a number of years. Without the audience getting what was communicated, it would not have existed for so long, right? Yes. That is right! But, this style of presentation is perhaps suited for presenting achievements, such as in weekly, monthly, and other governance meetings. In this type of meeting, the audience is present as the governance mandates them to be, and they probably have to answer questions posed to them at the most.

If we are getting into a presentation where the audience have to be equally involved in the creative process, involved in understanding what the content is all about, it is time to improvise and move into a better version of presenting content—the cognitive approach which is discussed in the next section.

Cognitive content

I read plenty of self-help books. A theme that I find common in most books is the way they present the data. The content within the binds of the book is valuable if and only if the reader is self-motivated to stay up and follow the prescription. So, it is imperative that self-help books must not be designed in a traditional way which introduces the agenda and takes us through one topic after another. Readers will not be compelled to follow through and the book will end up in the attic.

In self-help books (and in some business books too), they create hunger that coerces the reader to want to read the book. It creates a connection that allures the reader all the way to the end, and in most cases, the objective of being a best-selling book will be achieved thanks to the magnetism effect. We can very well replicate this style into presentations and make them engaging and connect with the audience. I call it cognitive content as opposed to traditional as we will be feeding the brain sufficient reasons to follow up and then hook onto the content.

Step 1 – Provide reasons why the presentation is worth the time and effort

In the presentation, the first step must always be to entice the audience into connecting with the material on display. The audience must understand how the presentation is going to help them succeed, get things done, or achieve the objectives as put forth by you. The reasons you provide must be valid and believable.

For example, if I was to build a presentation on the importance of communication in work life, I would probably state the following reasons in this section:

➤ Good communication helps you put across ideas effectively and efficiently

➤ It can potentially help you catapult your career into higher realms

➤ Higher customer satisfaction

➤ Better utilization of time

Make sure that the reasons you provide are convincing enough to evince interest in the presentation that follows.

Step 2 – Getting into the crux of the subject matter

In this section of the presentation, you will define the concepts, state detailed descriptions, introduce processes, and go as deep as you can. Remember that unless and until you justify what you state in this section with figures, stats, experiences, facts, specifications, and analysis, the audience are going to find it harder to intake the material that you are presenting.

Organize this section logically and sequentially. If you are running a presentation on driving a car, first introduce all the various controls like the gear stick, steering wheel, accelerator pedal, brake pedal, and the clutch pedal. Then start with the combinations that make driving possible. Go step by step. Sit in the shoes of the audience and visualize whether what is being presented makes sense to someone who is new to the subject matter.

Take a look at this book. I started with the basics of communication and then started to move in with written, telephonic, and face-to-face communication. Once I had the verbal and nonverbal communications laid out, I moved into presenting, and in the following chapter, I will discuss reports, business cases, and proposals. You can see me changing gears and going deeper as the book progresses. Replicate this in your presentation under this section and the audience will find it easy to follow you.

Step 3 – Application of subject matter to work life

The next section must provide direct application to one's work life if you are presenting in a work environment on a topic related to work. Similarly, if you are presenting on building better relationships with friends and family, it applies to all areas of life where friends and family intersect us.

For example, if I am presenting on the importance of communication, I would provide the following areas where it can be tested and verified:

➤ Next time you sit in a meeting, make sure your hands are in the region of your tummy and very much visible.

➤ When you draft e-mails, make sure you run spell check before hitting send.

➤ Put on a friendly tone every time you pick up the phone and speak into it.

➤ Use Microsoft's PowerPoint application for preparing slides. The application is easy to use and the output looks professional with a small learning curve.

Get the idea? Relate it directly to something that can be tried out practically. Make sure that this is not at an abstract level. Bringing in practicality after going deeper into the topic will help audience apply it in their daily lives and not just remember what was said but experience the presentation physically.

Step 4 – Q&A, summary, and conclusion

Ending a presentation is as important as starting one. Different speakers have different ways of doing it. Some sow thoughts relating to the subject matter that will make the audience think post presentation, some will ask the audience to come out with all the possible questions for instant clarification, and others suggest the next steps for the audience to take. There is no right or wrong way to end a presentation. Perhaps a combination of all three types will serve the audience best. Once again, the style of conclusion solely depends on the subject and the speaker.

In this book, I have spoken about a number of aspects in communication in IT work life. But, is it comprehensive? No. My conclusion will revolve around the leftover topics that will be picked up in my upcoming book. My point is that every context is different. If this book was the third or the fifth book in the series and I had nothing else to cover, I would perhaps ask the reader to act as a mentor to others around.

When you end a presentation, make sure that the audience does not have too many basic questions lingering around. If you want them to think about the topic after you are done presenting, it should be along the lines of—how else do you think we could have achieved it? If we are going to apply this to a different system, how would the test results look? Clarify basic questions, give something to ponder over, and most importantly, show them the path they need to pick up after your presentation. The audience does not like to get into a tunnel and find dead ends. Show the light and lead them to newer heights. For example, if you are running training on Microsoft Windows 7, tell them the next thing they need to learn after mastering Windows 7 is Microsoft Server 2010.

Also, while you end the presentation, make sure you run a slide summarizing the various topics the presentation has run through. This will help the audience recollect and perhaps ask you clarifying questions.

Action Point

Exercise (for readers to attempt at the end of this topic followed by a group discussion):

- Go through your presentation slides from the past, and it is likely that the presentation is based on the traditional approach. Is the presentation enticing enough to keep the audience glued?
- Discuss with the group on how these presentations can be modified based on the cognitive approach to make them more appealing.

Delivering effective and efficient presentations

Before we end this chapter, I want to provide you a set of pointers for delivering presentations successfully. Delivery of presentations is a huge topic by itself. So, the list I am about to provide may not be comprehensive, but it is sufficient for you to get started on the road to becoming a great presenter. Some of them may be repeats from earlier in the book and the chapter:

1. Practice delivering in front of a mirror if you can. Do a full rehearsal at least once and multiple rehearsals of parts that are difficult.

2. If you are able to get access to the room where you would be rehearsing beforehand, get to it and imagine an audience while you rehearse.

3. It is important that you look into finer aspects such as how you face the screen and at what angle you would face the audience.

4. Become familiar with the remote presenters and other equipment which you will employ throughout the presentation. If you end up learning the art during the session, you will lose the plot.

5. Through the most part of the presentation, your hands must be in the area of your belly to look trustworthy.

6. You may have great content projected on the screen, but if you don't build a connection with the audience, you will most likely not succeed in achieving the objectives.

7. Opening statements in a presentation must be enthusiastic, powerful, and must be aimed at connecting with the audience. As most of you have heard the phrase, first impressions last forever!

8. Make eye contact with your audience. You may not be able to cover everyone, but a sample number in every direction is good enough.

9. Clarify at the beginning whether you would like to be interrupted with questions or whether you would be taking them at the end.

10. Close your presentation with confidence and with thoughts that will linger on the audience's mind post the presentation.

Summary

As this chapter ends, you are expected to know the following:

> Different types of presentations and how each type differs in the way the presenter prepares and delivers the presentation

> The four pillars of presentation

> Understanding the objective of a presentation as a precursor to preparation

> Importance of analyzing audience before creating presentation material

> The tree-step approach to creating presentation slides

> How good speakers differentiate themselves from ordinary ones and other general tips on delivering presentations

> Tips on how to control nervousness

> The importance of becoming familiar with gadgets employed during presenting such as remote presenter, projector, screen, and microphone

> The different ways presentation material can be created

> The cognitive approach to creating content

In *Chapter 8, Reports, Proposals, and Business Cases*, we will look at how you can go about preparing reports in the most logical manner. We will also break down business proposals and how they need to be developed to get the attention of prospective customers. And finally, we will learn how to prepare business cases.

> 8

Reports, Proposals, and Business Cases

In this chapter, we will delve deeper into written forms of communication. I will discuss the various nuggets that need to be considered while preparing reports, provide pointers for creating proposals, and aid you in the preparation of business cases.

Basically, these three types of documents are applications of written communication. It is employed in different cases, although you might be fighting in your mind that a proposal and a business case could mean the same thing. They are not. You will find out the differences later on in this chapter.

In organizations, information exchanges happen mainly in the meeting rooms and over telephones. When the information in the picture relates to sensitive information such as performance, analysis, and new business, business leaders prefer to read it out of a formal document—such as reports, proposals, and business cases. They have their place in any organization, be it IT or non-IT. They are the major drivers for decision making in organizations and hence find a special place in the communication context.

The objective of these written forms is to highlight achievements or throw light on a problem which necessitates action. It gives leverage to the decision makers to make the right choices and understand the project from the operations to the contractual obligations. All businesses, projects, and teams require reports, proposals, and business cases for their sustenance. A poorly developed report or a business case will show an inaccurate picture of how the organization is performing and does not throw light on the critical aspects of the organization, which leads to poor decision making, and this cascades down to the organization's performance, turnover, and image.

Reports

Reports relay data based on facts and figures to aid in (business) decision making. They are a snapshot of information in a presentable and easily digestible format. Preparing effective reports is an art, and good reporting analysts and managers are in demand across various IT sectors.

In the IT field, there are several types of reports, and the list grows by the hour. Some popular types of reports include weekly status reports, service delivery reports, time tracking reports, project reports, and technical reports, among others. In fact, an organization can come up with a report that is probably unheard of in the industry. In one of the organizations that I was associated with, a team manager used to send out desktop performance reports of all his subordinates to the senior manager in order to convince them that the team needed better infrastructure. He came up with a formula to calculate what percentage of productivity was impacted due to obsolete desktops.

In this chapter, I will provide you with a high-level overview of how to go about preparing reports.

Importance of reports

In any organization, performance is key. All deciding factors and changes depend on performance. If any organization is doing very well, then the decision makers could turn their focus towards acquisition of clients. And if an organization is performing below par, then they could focus towards improving the designs, operations, and processes to bring the performance above the threshold. What makes these decision makers cognizant of a company's performance? Reports. Whether the intended area is profits/losses, contractual service level agreement compliance, customer feedback, or employee satisfaction—all these flavors are drawn up in the form of reports. The decision makers with the aid of reports can make judgment calls that either make or break the company. A good and accurate report will generally help in good decision making.

Let me strengthen the importance of reports with an example. A recently concluded employee survey mostly pointed towards employees asking for more annual leave days to use during sickness. The CEO of the company asked the reporting manager about the highlights of the feedback. The reporting manager felt that the feedback pertaining to sick leave was trivial and omitted it from the report. The CEO prepared his speech for the town hall session based on the decisions taken from the feedback. The failure to address employee concerns impacted the company's employee survey engagement score and thus the company became anything but first preference for good workers looking to change, and top-ranking graduate students. What is the root cause of this defacing image? Reports! An accurate and well-developed report could have turned the fortunes of the company's image around.

Process for reporting

The following flow chart shows the process of reporting:

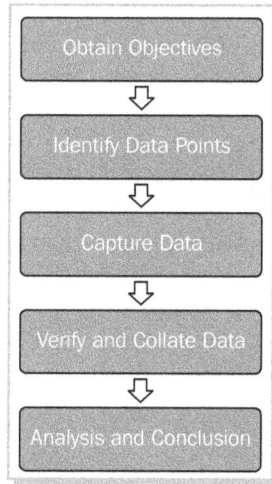

Step 1 – Obtain objectives

In this book, you might have observed that we dig right down to the source of the problem that we are trying to alleviate in order to come up with a solution. In reporting too, we adopt a similar strategy. We first need to understand the purpose of preparing the report that we are entrusted with. So, before you begin with the actual development of the report, ask yourself the question—what purpose am I going to serve through this report or what is the objective that I need to achieve through the report? Answers could vary between the sun and the moon. As long as you are able to question the intent and articulate an answer that can be translated into relevant reports, your job of preparing effective reports is on course.

Let's say that you are asked to prepare a team productivity report by your manager. So, how would you start? Find out why your manager requires this report. Does he want to keep a finger on the pulse of how his team are performing, whether he is scaling the team for additional workload, or is he looking at productivity improvement opportunities? Knowing the objective will help you prepare the report from a certain angle, which is desirable.

Step 2 – Identify data points

When you enquire with your manager about the objectives, you understand that your manager wants to know how utilized the team members are and whether the team strength can be optimized to effect financial cutbacks. So, the next step in formulating the report is to identify the data points—various sets of information that you would require in order to draw up a report and their respective sources. You may require multiple types of information, which involves single or most likely multiple sources that can feed accurate data. To state some examples of sources—you might have a project management tool to keep track of what activity is getting done and who is working on it, you might have an online work-tracking tool in the form of tickets, or you might have team calendars for tracking meetings and e-mails.

If you are looking to prepare a report on IT infrastructure such as a server, you may just have a single source in a performance-monitoring engine. In short, every report is different. Some may have a single data point and most have multiple ones. The trick is to identify all the available sources to ensure that the report is comprehensive and accurate.

Step 3 – Capture data

You have identified the data points and the next logical step is to start capturing the generated data. You will need data for a certain period of time for the law of averages to work its magic. The timeframe that is needed for pulling meaningful reports is a call that is to be taken on a case-by-case basis.

You can capture data either manually or employ automated tools if available. For the server performance monitoring report I stated earlier, you could automate it. There are tools available that help you automate the capturing process. If the option is available, use it. If not, you will have to get back to manual methods of capturing data—as in data from e-mails, calendars, and so on. This is cumbersome and prone to errors. When there are no automation options, you just need to understand the challenges with manual capture and take extra precaution in ensuring accurate data for your report.

If you are relying on keying in the data manually by referring to the source such as the e-mail, the likelihood of errors creeping in is more. Suppose you are preparing a report on your subordinates who responded to a feedback survey over an e-mail. You want to tabulate the findings and present it to your bosses. Since you sought the feedback over an e-mail, you are left with no option but to manually key in the answers into your report. In this case, you would open every e-mail and populate the corresponding information onto a tabulation sheet such as an MS Excel spreadsheet. You do this work trusting what you see and what you key in are one and the same. We are creatures of emotion, so it is possible that we may key in inaccurate data in the tabulation while we are stressed or while our mind drifts onto future appointments and travel plans. A better option in this case would have been to develop the feedback system on a website and tabulate the results directly from the website. This would have saved a whole bunch of time, and more importantly, it would have been error-free.

Step 4 – Verify and collate data

Never ever accept data without verifying the correctness of it. Check and double check, especially if you are capturing it manually. If automation is employed, verify with the source whether what is generated and what is reported are one and the same.

One of the ways to verify data is to compare data from multiple sources. Suppose you are capturing data from a project management tool. It is possible that the same data can be fetched from another source. If you have that luxury, double check the accuracy of the data by running a comparison with the two sets. An example could be the data pulled from a website hosting feedback surveys and comparing it with the acknowledgement received from project team members over e-mails.

You might have captured the data for a week, a fortnight, or a month. Put it together so that you can trend, analyze, and come out with your conclusions.

Step 5 – Analysis and conclusion

In the reporting process, analysis and conclusion is perhaps the most interesting section. Here, you could play judge by reading the trends and coming out with your opinion.

If I am working on mainly numbers, I generally put down everything onto an Excel sheet and use the inbuilt pivot feature available on Microsoft Excel to filter and represent data that makes sense to the reader. It is a powerful tool, and if you aren't familiar with it already, I recommend that you learn it; the learning curve is fairly short.

You can employ charts for displaying trends on how the productivity has improved (or gone down) over a period, segregate the type of work carried out in a pie chart, or use a Gantt chart for showcasing project schedules. There are multiple options available. You just have to choose the one apt for your case.

If you are working on discrete data which is not in the form of numbers like customer feedback comments or audit findings, you should come up with meaningful analysis and reasonable conclusions and display it in a visual layout if possible. Remember that visual appeal adds to the data you are trying to convey, especially in reports.

Action Point

Exercise (for students to attempt at the end of this topic followed by a group discussion):

Identify all the reports that are in vogue in your team/organization. For every report, analyze whether the report is being true to its objectives, whether it is capturing all the possible data sources, and whether the data is being verified before getting published.

Business proposals

Organizations need to grow; they need to get new customers to survive against the cutthroat competition that the world presents. In IT, the competition is fierce, with a number of startup players springing up. An IT service provider or a product developer can get business by showcasing the skills, products, and processes that the company possesses at their disposal. A proposal is a formal written document which is a powerful tool in presenting and selling your services and products to prospective customers. In this section, I will go through high-level topics on how a business proposal must look and the various topics that make it up.

Importance of business proposals

Let me put it this way. You cannot do away with the formality of developing and presenting business proposals to prospective clients. You might present about a wonderful business idea to a client with a well thought out presentation and corroborated facts. The prospective client could be as eager as a beaver during the presentation, and that could give you the vibes that he is in on your idea. But, it is a fact of business that the client wants to see the thoughts and facts in black and white so he or she can verify, share, think over, and compare at the comfort of their office or home, and not in a conference room.

Let's say in another instance, you didn't get the time to present your product or service to a prospective customer. He asked you to send in a business proposal. Think of this business proposal as a great marketing tool that you could use in presenting the strong points of your products, the achievements of your company, how your company differentiates itself from others in the market, and all the other topics that make your product stand out from the rest. This powerful marketing tool is making your life easy. You are not required to travel to be able to present for this meeting, you are not required to block your time, and most importantly, you can replicate the business proposal to any number of prospective clients. In other words, you can make better work of your time rather than repeating yourself to every client. A powerful business proposal can do it for you instead!

An unstated importance of business proposals is a matter of formality and compliance. Client companies these days like to retain business proposals in their repositories for a number of reasons. It could be that they would like to keep a record of what was promised and what was delivered, their internal processes mandate them to retain all proposals, or certain external certifications could mandate retaining proposals. Government organizations especially need to retain all business proposals—including the ones that they did not entertain for the sake of picking a winner amongst multiple product vendors.

The language

The audience for a business proposal are key decision makers who more often than not will not necessarily be technical people. So, in essence, a business proposal must do away with the jargon, and be drafted with simple everyday language. The writing must conform to all the 7 C's of communication that we discussed in *Chapter 2, From Governance to Communication*.

Along with the words, adorn your proposal with images and visuals to drive the core message to your audience. Remember that the objective of a proposal is to let your prospective buyer know what you can do for them, and putting this across in a simple, nonconvoluted, and uncomplicated manner does the trick.

Save the best for the first

Whenever we write, the general format we use is to introduce the topic in the first couple of paragraphs and move into the meat of the topic after and then add the conclusion, which is where the core message is stationed. Now, in a business proposal, you just need to reverse everything. You are trying to sell your services or product to the customer, and the proposal will aid the customer in making an informed decision. So, it is your prerogative to win over the customer at the earliest.

In a proposal, you must begin pitching your products and services from the very first section. Give the customer a good reason to read further. Don't assume that yours is the only proposal that they have to play with; I mentioned the competition earlier, so expect the customer to have a number of proposals on hand for evaluating and making a decision.

Communicate to the customer why your company is the best in line to meet the customer's requirements and highlight your company's strengths and allay fears that they may have regarding your credentials. Let them know about your company, achievements, certifications, clientele list, and customer feedback comments in the first few sections. Keep the mundane stuff like the process, methodology, and price to the second half of the document.

The proposal preparation

Prospective customers put down their requirements in a document called a **Request for Proposal** (**RFP**)—technical, functional, and operational requirements. The document also contains information on who can bid—meaning minimum qualification for companies to enter the bidding process.

Prospective bidders must fully understand the RFP document to be in a position to come with a solution for the customer's requirements and to quote a competitive price for the products or services offered. You need to research the client and correlate the requirements. In many cases, what the customer says they want on a RFP document and what they actually need are two different things.

Extensive research from your end and asking relevant questions to the client will unravel the exact nature of the problem. And, knowing this as accurately as possible is the best tool you can hope for in winning over the contract. It is also recommended that you speak to the client directly to understand the requirements rather than taking the RFP at face value. Also, you may choose to talk to different people in the organization to triangulate on the requirements.

Let's say that you are convinced that you understand your client's problem fully and completely. You will need to build a solution to solve the problem. You need a methodology to help you arrive at the solution. This section is technical in nature, and you must be absolutely sure that the proposed solution works for the client, and it delivers on all its promises. Remember that based on your solution, the costing gets impacted. So, be doubly sure about the solution you are going in for.

The proposal format

There are a number of ways to structure a proposal document. The objective is to catch the interest of the client and to get them interested in the content and your credentials. As I mentioned earlier, I believe in putting the best foot forward and then coming up with the mundane and necessary information.

This is the format I propose:

1. Executive summary introducing your company along with the credentials, how your company is best suited to alleviate the client's problem, and how the customer can benefit by partnering with you.

2. Summarize the customer's requirements as you understand it. Keep it to the point, as the customer may just be interested in seeing whether you understood the requirements.

3. In brief, explain what you are going to do, and how you are going to help the customer in achieving their objectives.

4. Provide a detailed methodology; the process you are going to follow and the specifics of the solution that you are going to employ. If you can visualize it with boxes, arrows, shapes, and figures, it enhances the value of the message.

5. Provide a staffing plan on the technical experts who would be a part of this project and highlight their credentials. Remember that you are selling, and you need to highlight the assets that you own, and human assets are the most sought after.

6. Provide the timelines that you need to achieve the intended output and the associated costs. The costing process must be done transparently and by tagging it directly to the methodology. For example, if you have a ten-step methodology, calculate how many hours you need for every step and factor in the per hour rate to come up with the total cost of the project.

7. Garnish the proposal by listing down the benefits of the recommended solution and how you can further improve it. Remember, you are already pitching in for the next in line project as well.

Sample business proposal

I have included a sample business proposal to bring in the sense of how the theory that I discussed previously looks in flesh and bones. In the strictest sense, the business proposal that I have given next is a sample one. It is extremely rare that a business proposal can be as concise and as simple as the one to follow. It normally ranges upwards of 30-40 pages, and contains a number of sections that I have indicated in the proposal format sub-topic.

In the sample, the IT service company Servicer is trying to pitch to take over Client business services' call center division.

Objective

Client business services is the fastest growing professional services organization. It intends to support its customers with a call center which is available round the clock and provide solutions instantly.

Requirement 1 : Set up a call center that is available 24X7, including public holidays

Requirement 2 : Provide administrative support in professional services to its selective list of customers

Requirement 3 : Introduce the services to prospective clients

About Company Servicer

Servicer was set up in the year 1997 by a group of IT experts. The company has 10,000 employees spread across 25 locations worldwide. The company is headquartered in London, UK. We were one of the pioneers of outsourcing the call center industry in the late nineties and we serve close to 200 customers in Europe, North America and Australia.

Focus Area

Servicer had a series of discussions with Client business services' senior vice president Mark Head and his team to understand the shortcomings that company is facing and to understand the activities that you wish to outsource.

Client business services has over 100,000 customers worldwide who would require instant support across timezones. The focus areas for us is to support your customers and continue the services that you were providing to them. Additionally, you want us to generate sales by cold calling and selling services when prospective customers dial in.

Approach

At a high level, we propose to solution as below:

- Study the company offered services in detail and prepare a plan for transition.
- Identify core team within Servicer who would serve as the interface between Client business services and Servicer.
- Transition knowledge, tools, accesses, IT infrastructure among others to Servicer.

Staffing

- We enjoy a bench strength of over 75 employees who can get empowered to work on Client business services' activities within a month.
- Hiring will begin immediately, and within the first month and a half, we should be fully staffed.
- Simultaneously, we will try to move some employees working on other accounts to Client business services.

Timelines and Investment

Timelines

- Preparation : 1 week
- Study and Planning : 3 weeks
- Transition to offshore : 3 weeks

Investment

- With Purchase Order : $750,000
- 25% Completion of Transition : $500,000
- 100% Completion of Transition : $750,000
- Ongoing Monthly : $900,000

Queries

Please direct all your queries regarding the proposal to our business development team : business.development@servicer.com.

Action Point

Exercise (for students to attempt at the end of this topic followed by a group discussion):

You have been asked to respond to a bid with a business proposal highlighting your achievements and the solution that you have worked out for the customer. It is a consulting project that requires oversight of activities specific to your domain and the length of the project is six months. Prepare a proposal selling your services to the customer, and giving them ample reasons for picking you over the others.

Business cases

Business cases are documents that argue for a specific action, and provide substantiations, rationales, justifications, and other support in order to compel the sponsor into taking a desired action.

Business cases are mostly drafted for commercial purposes where you have an amount getting invested, and the business goes into justifying the investment and coming up with the return on investment. For example, if you are going to invest X amount of money into a project, sub project, or a new business, how much time will it take for you to recover the money and what is the rate of profit you would start seeing thereafter?

In IT, we write business cases all the time, depending on the domain you are in. Some commercial business cases include setting up a monitoring system for automatic detection and notification, procuring faster laptops, and setting up applications for generating reports. In each of these cases, you can potentially show how investing a certain amount of money can lead to benefits which reduce the human effort, reduces errors, and increases productivity.

You can write noncommercial business cases as well. It simply means that there is no money invested into a decision, but rather a change in the way we work. You could be writing a business for reorganizing teams—thereby providing the positive effects it can have on the team, delivery, morale, and logistical optimization, among others. Basically, as I mentioned earlier, you will have a problem statement which the business case attends to, provides a solution, justifies the solution, tallies cost against benefits, and argues with the sponsor for going in with the decision.

So, a commercial business case involves investing money, and the end results generally expect to see a return on investment like a company investing X dollars and expecting to see 2X or 3X within a certain period of time. Or the expected end result could be customer perception/satisfaction or complying with a legal obligation. In a noncommercial business case, the changes specified in the business case do not involve money. That said, the changes are not superficial either. The changes that are being justified involve noncommercial elements that make up an organization and its services.

Elements of a business case

A business case is a document where you put in a compelling case for a decision to be taken in your favor. So, in this document, you can add whatever you need to convince the reader of the benefits and the actions to be taken. But, there are certain generic elements that are accepted to be pretty standard in a business case, and I will present them to you in brief.

Before you start to put pen on paper, you need to ensure that you have the key items for all the sections that I mention next. You need to have done the research and have the substantiating information to complete the elements of a business case.

Problem statement

What are you trying to solve through this business case? The decision you are aiming for must be targeted towards something—like nonproductivity through slow laptops, disintegrating the team due to a weak matrix organization, or lack of Internet bandwidth to carry out daily operations. In short, you need to know what you are going to attack. This is along the same lines of what I have been discussing all along in this book: *know the objective you are trying to achieve.*

Problem analysis

In the problem statement, you don't go into details. You just state a high-level problem—like what you see from 40,000 feet. In the problem analysis section, you get into specifics. You go into minute details of what you think is the problem and what are the ill effects of living with the problem. You can go into as many items as you want; the sponsor might choose to read it or skip it, but the information has to be there if he or she chooses the former.

Assumptions

Before you come up with a solution, you would have assumed certain things like the rate of inflation in the next five years, future customer requirements, and so on. Put down all the assumptions you have made so there is a transparency you are creating for the reader to see and believe what they are reading. At the end of the day, if you are going to say that the business will grow by 20% year on year, the substantiation must justify your numbers, and numbers are generally an outcome of market situations, changes in technology, and customer focus, among others. Remember that your justifications must not sound like a car salesman plucking random numbers from the air and making a mountain out of a mouse.

Solution

The solution to the problem on hand must be down as clear as day. If you can provide multiple solution options, it provides a wider array of decisions to make. When you provide a solution, you can explain how it works using visuals, support theories using graphs, and come up with whatever form of written communication that you need to subscribe to in order to make your point.

Cost-benefit analysis

This is the section that talks about the moolah. Simply put, you would estimate the cost of the solution and list down the benefits you are getting out of the solution. Later you would map the cost against the benefits to prove that the benefits exceed the cost of the solution. In business language, we call it **return on investment (ROI)** and **value on investment (VOI)**.

Recommendations

In most cases, you would have come up with multiple solution options. So, in recommendations, you can write what you feel that the sponsor must opt for. You are giving your two cents, against the solutions handpicked by you.

I recommend that we purchase an off the shelf portal software and customize it for our needs. My research has come up with XYZ software and our team has the skills to customize it.

You will also recommend how you want the project to be scheduled, the people who are needed to be involved, and the disbursement of funds. You can reiterate the problem, solution, and the cost-benefit analysis yet again to bring in clarity to the concluding section of the business case.

Business case template

Here is the table of contents for a typical business case. Feel free to add additional fields. Remember that the objective is to convince the sponsor to sway in your direction.

The executive summary is a high-level view of what the business case contains. You will introduce the problem statement, speak on the cost-benefit analysis, and discuss the recommendations in plain business language. In this section, you will stay away from all technical lingo.

Comparison with competition is self-explanatory. To put up a compelling argument, it helps in knowing what the competition does, and when the competition employ a certain solution, it is proof that it will work, and the sponsors would be all the more likely to give it a nod.

You can put in a detailed list of project activities along with the timelines that the activities will take. You can also put down the cost of every activity, the risks and challenges involved, and just about all the project information that you feel the need to share. The more the better as long as it is accurate.

Sample business case

You can find a sample IT business case in this section. You will observe that it is a lot smaller than the business proposal. Generally, that is how it is in the real IT world.

Executive Summary

Tabulating the outage data for customer King LLC shows that in the past 12 months we have had 342 outages, and on 10 occasions we did not meet the SLA targets and have been penalized $450,000.

We have performed detailed investigation on the nature of the outages and their root causes. We have identified that the infrastructure we manage is unreliable due to the technology, age and the architecture. To mitigate the issue, we have come up with the following solutions:

- Refresh the infrastructure that is older than 5 years and move to newer and stable technologies. Cost of project $3 million.
- Implement monitoring systems so that we are alerted as soon as there is an outage and we get a fair chance of restoring the service before the SLA targets. Cost of project $600,000.

The first solution is risky considering that the contract with the customer ends in the next 30 months. The second solution involving monitoring systems seems to be a pragmatic one considering that we could possible estimate saving $500,000 before the contract is due for renewal. If we are able to restore the services without breaching the SLAs, there is an excellent opportunity that King LLC would continue working with us, and we can promise them a complete infrastructure refresh.

Problem Statement

The IT infrastructure for King LLC was transitioned to us when we acquired the company Taken Pvt Ltd. The infrastructure along with the architecture, applications and processes were taken over by us in verbatim. Over the years, we have made changes to the way we work but not to the IT infrastructure. The applications leveraged are over the hill and other organizations have retired these applications for newer technologies. The inadequate infrastructure is unreliable and has been the cause of 80% of the outages, and all the SLA breaches are attributed towards infrastructure failure.

Solution

We have identified two alternatives to mitigate the outages due to infrastructure:

- Refresh the infrastructure that is older than 5 years and move to newer and stable technologies.
- Implement monitoring systems so that we are alerted as soon as there is an outage and we get a fair chance of restoring the service before the SLA targets.

Cost Benefit Analysis

Solution	Cost of Investment (USD)	Yearly Saving (USD)	ROI
Refresh Infrastructure	3000000	450000	16 months
Implement Monitoring	600000	700000	50 months

- If we are to refresh the infrastructure, we will invest $3 million and the yearly saving that we can expect is $700,000 considering that we can save the SLA breaches and the number of employees which is an advantage that new infrastructure brings about. Return on investment is a little over 4 years.
- Implementing monitoring would be a smaller project at $450,000 and we are confident that we could save the SLA breaches but we need to continue with the current employee strength to achieve the savings. Return on investment is around 16 months.

Recommendation

The first solution is risky considering that the contract with the customer ends in the next 30 months. The second solution involving monitoring systems seems to be a pragmatic one considering that we could possible estimate saving $500,000 before the contract is due for renewal. If we are able to restore the services without breaching the SLAs, there is an excellent opportunity that King LLC would continue working with us, and we can promise them a complete infrastructure refresh.

Action Point

Exercise (for students to attempt at the end of this topic followed by a group discussion):

Identify an improvement opportunity in your project/team/organization and prepare a business case based on the input provided in this chapter. Obtain feedback from your manager about whether the case you have put up is compelling enough for action to be taken.

Summary

As this chapter ends, you are expected to know the following:

➤ Objectives of reports and the importance of developing reports

➤ Process for preparing reports

➤ Difference between business proposals and business cases

➤ Structure of business proposals and how you can go about constructing one

➤ Structure of business cases and how you can go about constructing one

www.ingramcontent.com/pod-product-compliance
Lightning Source LLC
Chambersburg PA
CBHW080555220326
41599CB00032B/6494